THE RIGHTS OF SUSPECTS

THE AMERICAN CIVIL LIBERTIES UNION HANDBOOK SERIES

AN AMERICAN
CIVIL LIBERTIES
UNION HANDBOOK

THE
RIGHTS OF
SUSPECTS

Oliver Rosengart
with GAIL WEINHEIMER

General Editors of this series:
Norman Dorsen, *General Counsel*
Aryeh Neier, *Executive Director*
Special Editor:
Ruth Bader Ginsburg, *Coordinator,*
   ACLU Women's Rights Project

A Richard Baron Book
Sunrise Books, Inc. / E. P. Dutton & Co., Inc.

Published simultaneously in Canada by Clarke, Irwin & Company
Limited, Toronto and Vancouver

ISBN: 0-87690-138-0
Library of Congress Catalog Number: 74-76009

TABLE OF CONTENTS

Preface

This guide sets forth your rights under present law and offers suggestions on how you can protect your rights. It is one of a series of guidebooks published in cooperation with the American Civil Liberties Union on the rights of teachers, servicemen, mental patients, prisoners, students, criminal suspects, women, and the very poor.

The hope surrounding these publications is that Americans informed of their rights will be encouraged to exercise them. Through their exercise, rights are given life. If they are rarely used, they may be forgotten and violations may become routine.

This guide offers no assurances that your rights will be respected. The laws may change and, in some of the subjects covered in these pages, they change quite rapidly. An effort has been made to note those parts of the law where movement is taking place but it is not always possible to predict accurately when the law *will* change.

Even if the laws remain the same, interpretations of them by courts and administrative officials often vary. In a federal system such as ours, there is a built-in problem of the differences between state and federal law, not to speak of the confusion of the differences from state to state. In addition, there are wide variations in the ways in which particular courts and administrative officials will interpret the same law at any given moment.

If you encounter what you consider to be a specific abuse of your rights you should seek legal assistance. There are a number of agencies that may help you, among them ACLU affiliate offices, but bear in mind that the ACLU is a limited-purpose organization. In many communities, there are federally funded legal service offices which provide assistance to poor persons who cannot afford the costs of legal representation. In general, the rights that the ACLU defends are freedom of inquiry and expression; due process of law; equal protection of the laws; and privacy. The authors in this series have discussed other rights in these books (even though they sometimes fall outside the ACLU's usual concern) in order to provide as much guidance as possible.

These books have been planned as guides for the people directly affected: therefore the question and answer format. In some of these areas there are more detailed works available for "experts." These guides seek to raise the largest issues and inform the non-specialist of the basic law on the subject. The authors of the books are themselves specialists who understand the need for information at "street level."

No attorney can be an expert in every part of the law. If you encounter a specific legal problem in an area discussed in one of these guidebooks, show the book to your attorney. Of course, he will not be able to rely *exclusively* on the guidebook to provide you with adequate representation. But if he hasn't had a great deal of experience in the specific area, the guidebook can provide some helpful suggestions on how to proceed.

Norman Dorsen, General Counsel
American Civil Liberties Union

Aryeh Neier, Executive Director
American Civil Liberties Union

Introduction

The Fifth and Fourteenth Amendments to the United States Constitution guarantee to everyone in this country the right not to be deprived of life, liberty or property without due process of law. "Due process of law" means that the state—police, prosecutors and courts—must follow certain rules and procedures in investigating, charging and trying people for crimes. Most of these rules are established by the Bill of Rights. For example, the Fourth Amendment prohibits searches by the police without a warrant; the Fifth Amendment guarantees the right of a person not to be forced to testify against himself; the Sixth Amendment guarantees the right not to be tried without a lawyer; and the Eighth Amendment prohibits cruel and unusual punishment. These principles are basic and easy to understand. The difficulty comes in figuring out exactly how they apply in specific situations. While everyone agrees that a person being tried for a crime should have a lawyer, there are, for example, disagreements about when that right begins—at trial? at the arrest? before the arrest? These are the kinds of questions that courts have been asked to decide in literally thousands of cases.

13

This book does not attempt to discuss all of the rights that suspects and defendants have throughout the entire criminal process. Rather it concentrates on the rights of persons before they have been charged with a crime, when they are arrested and up until the time they finally go to trial. Another book in this series will take up the rights of defendants during and after trial.

Throughout the text of this book you will see references to court cases by name and followed by numbers and letters, for example, *Davis v. Mississippi*, 394 U.S. 721 (1969). The first number refers to the volume of a series of books. The letters refer to the series. (U.S. means the series in which Supreme Court opinions appear; F., F.2d and F. Supp refer to the series of books containing Federal Court opinions; and state court cases have state abbreviations such as N.Y., Mass., and Tex.) The final number is the page on which the case appears; the year the case was decided (and sometimes letters referring to the particular branch of the court) is in parenthesis at the end. Thus, *Davis v. Mississippi* is on page 721 of volume 394 of the United States Reports and was decided in 1969. Many large libraries have these books and law schools will often let outsiders use their libraries.

I

Rights in Individual Confrontations With the Police

Our society is only as free as the local cop on the beat makes it free, and he makes it much freer for the middle- or upper-class white than for everyone else. If you are on the fringes of society, if you are a hippie, a hobo, or just poor or black or brown, or if you have ever watched a cop deal with those outside the mainstream, you will probably have seen illegal police activity or perhaps just plain police harassment. It takes innumerable forms, from telling people who are hanging out on the street to move on, to stopping and questioning people, searching them, searching cars, and sometimes ordering people to get out of town, falsely arresting people, and occasionally beating and even robbing them. Most of this conduct is obviously illegal, but police engage in so much of it so often that many people erroneously think it is authorized by law. This chapter will attempt to set forth the law on what police can and cannot do in individual confrontations with people, and what can be done about police misconduct in this area.

STOP AND FRISK

When, in general, can the police conduct searches?

The Fourth Amendment to the United States Constitution protects all citizens from *unreasonable* searches and seizures by the government. The word "unreasonable" obviously does not tell us much, but the law that has developed in this area is that the police can search only: (1) with a warrant; (2) incident to a lawful arrest; or (3) upon consent of the person being searched. An arrest, and thus a search in connection with it, is lawful only where the police have *probable cause* to believe that a crime has been committed and that the defendant committed it. Using the words "probable cause" does not shed very much light on what is lawful, but more on that later.

Can the police do something less than search, without probable cause?

Yes. There is a level of police confrontation with citizens which is deemed less than a search and which need not meet the requirements of searches. It is commonly referred to as a "stop and frisk." The law in this area gives the police, upon *suspicion,* which is less than the probable cause needed to make an arrest and search, the authority to ask people for identification, to ask them what their business is in being where they are, and to pat down the outside of their clothing in a search for weapons if the policeman justifiably suspects that the person is armed. If the officer feels something that may be a weap-

18

on, he can then reach into the clothing for it (since he then has probable cause to believe that a crime—possession of a weapon—is being committed). If the citizen gives an explanation of his actions and has no weapon, he is legally free to leave. The officer is not permitted to extensively interrogate merely upon suspicion.

Eleven states have stop-and-frisk laws (see Table 1). Several of those states have laws authorizing questioning and searches more thorough than a frisk, which would seem to be unconstitutional. Eight other states—Delaware, Hawaii, Illinois, Louisiana, Massachusetts, Missouri, New Hampshire and Rhode Island—have another law called the Uniform Arrest Act. It allows the police to forcibly detain someone for up to two hours if he or she fails to identify himself or explain his actions to the satisfaction of the detaining officer. Only at the end of this period must he be released unless probable cause exists for arrest. Although some courts have upheld the practice, during the time of detention there are limits on what the police can do. A search greater than a frisk would seem to be illegal. Also, other evidence, like fingerprints, cannot be taken. In the case of *Davis v. Mississippi*, 394 U.S. 721 (1969), the Supreme Court held that a general roundup, followed by fingerprinting, of many young blacks in a small Southern town was illegal (no probable cause or even suspicion existed).

Table 1
Stop and Frisk Statutes

Alabama	Questioning and search for weapons.
Arkansas	15 minute limit; can only pat down for weapons; lists guidelines for "reasonable

	suspicion"; imposes civil liability for unlawful stop and frisk.
Illinois	Questioning and search for weapons.
Indiana	Questioning and pat down.
Kansas	Questioning and search.
Louisiana	Questioning and pat down.
Nevada	15 minute limit on questioning; search; person "shall not be compelled" to answer.
North Dakota	Questioning and search.
Utah	Questioning and search.
Wisconsin	Questioning and search.
New York	Upon suspicion police can question and pat down.

What if a citizen refuses to submit to a stop and frisk?

In those states having a stop and frisk law or Uniform Arrest Act, failing to submit to detention and frisk could result in an arrest. The situation would then be such that although the citizen's conduct was lawful, or only suspicious (anyone out very late at night is suspicious to some people), a mild resistance to the authority that questioned it could lead to a lawful arrest. As of early 1973, there is no Supreme Court case on this subject.

What about those states without stop-and-frisk or uniform arrest laws?

It would appear that, in an individual confrontation, a citizen could refuse to answer any questions asked by a police officer, refuse to show identification and walk away. Keep in mind that although your activity may be lawful it

20

may lead to being arrested and perhaps abused for committing what many policemen consider the sin of questioning a police officer's authority. Unless you want to risk arrest, it may be wiser to tell the officer that you believe that you are not required to answer his questions, that you are doing so under protest, but that you will answer his questions and show him identification just to be cooperative. You might want to note his name and badge number to make a complaint, but memorize it rather than writing it down in front of him or he will consider it a provocation, and you will certainly be hassled.

Do the same general limits apply to police behavior during roadblocks?

The roadblock is another form of brief detention, used to try to catch fleeing criminals: all the cars and trucks on the road are stopped and searched (a procedure that constitutes more than frisking) and the occupants of the vehicles may be briefly questioned. This practice entirely bypasses the constitutional requirements of probable cause for a search, and even suspicion for a frisk. Roadblocks have also been used to blockade certain areas of a city so that everyone going in and out could be detained and searched for weapons and contraband. Thus far there has been no Supreme Court decision on the constitutionality of these practices, although state courts usually uphold such measures. One Federal decision, *Bowling v. U.S.*, 350 F. 2d 1002 (1965), invalidated the practice where it was obviously used as a subterfuge to search for other reasons.

SEARCHES OF PERSONS

Illegal searches by the police in the United States are so much a part of regular police activity that one researcher found that the police still searched people illegally even though observers accompanied them on their rounds. In New York's Greenwich Village the Tactical Patrol Force regularly stops cars, orders the occupants out, searches the people and their car and sends them on their way if they are "clean." I have personally seen at least a dozen such illegal searches, without especially looking for them, in my own neighborhood. The stopping and illegal searching of individuals who are simply walking or standing on the street is even more common, and all illegal searches are much more frequent in the ghettoes than elsewhere. Usually the police simply order the person into a hallway and search there, but sometimes the search is conducted right out on the sidewalk and the individual is ordered to empty his pockets onto a car. Other variations on the theme include the victim being placed in a patrol car and searched while being driven around, or even being taken to the police station and stripped.

When are the police permitted to search persons on the street?

As mentioned in the previous section, only: (1) incident to a lawful arrest, which must be supported by probable cause to believe that the arrestee committed a crime; (2) with a search warrant; or (3) with the free and voluntary consent of the person being searched.

22

In actual practice, no warrant exists in the common confrontation between police and individual, in which the individual is simply searched. Free and voluntary consent seems practically impossible when the searcher is a policeman with a gun, and obviously no one who has anything to hide would freely consent to be searched. Some courts have recognized this logic. A heavy burden of proving consent is placed on the state where the state claims consent. In one case, *Kelly v. United States,* 111 U.S. App. D.C. 396 (1961), the defendant was sitting in a restaurant, two police officers asked him to step outside and when asked what he had in his pockets he admitted that he had marijuana. The court held that there was no consent. Thus arresting officers usually claim that street searches are incidental to a lawful arrest, although in fact the search usually comes first and the arrest later.

Are the results of an illegal search admissible as evidence in a trial?

No. In 1961 the Supreme Court decided the landmark case of *Mapp v. Ohio,* 367 U.S. 643 (1961), in which it held that the results of illegal searches were not admissible in state court trials. Prior to 1961 the results of illegal searches were inadmissible in federal court trials.

What do the police do to justify illegal searches?

They often lie. Usually they make up a story about how the arrest took place so it appears that there was probable cause to arrest before any search took place. One version is so common that it has a name: the "dropsy story." In it, the police officer says that as he approached the defendant, the accused threw contraband to the ground, and the police officer retrieved it without losing sight thereof, found it to be contraband and arrested the defendant. Although the dropsy story is occasionally true, it is usually used when the police have simply searched the defendant illegally; most possessors of contraband know better than to take it out of their pocket in front of a police officer. A study sponsored by Mobilization For Youth, an antipoverty program on New York's Lower East Side, found that there was a 60 percent increase in the frequency of dropsy stories after the Supreme Court held that the results of illegal searches are not admissible in state court trials.

There are many other variations on the dropsy theme. The police may claim that they saw the contraband in plain view, which gave them probable cause to arrest. They may say they saw a gun emerging from a belt or visible in an open handbag, or that they saw drugs being passed from one person to another or that they saw people using drugs. Sometimes the dropsy or plain-view stories are true, although it is common knowledge to everyone connected with law enforcement that police perjury in this area is very common.

Who decides whether an illegal search has taken place?

The judge, without a jury, prior to trial. The defendant must move to suppress the evidence on the ground that it was obtained as a result of an illegal search, and a hearing is then held. At this hearing, the police officer testifies and the defendant may testify. See Chapter III for further discussion.

What if you are walking along, stopped and ordered to empty your pockets?

Perhaps you can start by politely saying that you know that that is an illegal search, that you do not consent to such a search, but that you will not struggle if the police persist in ordering you to submit to the search. If the police persist, which they probably will, and if you have contraband on you, you should then start preparing for trial. If there are two police officers, get both badge numbers (but without writing them down, memorize them), since only one policeman will be the arresting officer and the other officer may be inconsistent in his testimony, which sheds doubt on the testimony of both. If the contraband was wrapped in something like a cigarette pack, an eyeglass case, or even paper, that can be helpful at a motion to suppress and you should try to retrieve any wrapping that the police leave behind. Most importantly, look around you for witnesses, even witnesses who just saw you go in and out of a building. If you can, tell your name to people standing nearby so that if anyone wants to, they will be able to find you. If you get out of jail come back to the scene as soon as possible, and if it is a residential neighborhood talk to people who hang around, visit all the apartments with windows that face the street and ask people if they saw you. If the scene of the arrest is a business area, it may be fruitful, if you know that some people saw the arrest, to distribute leaflets to passers-by who are on the street at approximately the same time of day that the arrest took place. Finding one independent witness, who does not know you and has no stake in the outcome, is something even the most biased judges find difficult to ignore.

How should you react if you witness what you think is an illegal search?

If you are with someone who gets searched, and perhaps you get searched too but nothing is found on you, stay cool and quiet. Do not argue the legality of the search with the police. You are a much more valuable witness if you are not arrested. If you protest at the time of the arrest, the police may think that you will make trouble for them, and they may arrest you and divide whatever contraband may have been found between you and the person you are with. As the Knapp Commission hearings into police corruption in New York have shown, and as many lawyers have observed in their practice, it is not rare for police to keep part of what they seize, especially when there is a large amount or it is of very high quality.

If you are witness to an illegal search, and an arrest follows, again it is wisest to stay calm, watch everything, make a mental note of all the details (testimony is generally more believable if detailed) and then write it all down as soon as possible after the incident. Any interference with the police, which might include saying even a few words to them, can lead to arrest on a charge of

26

interfering with an arrest. Whenever the police fear that a witness will report their misconduct, whether beating someone or illegally searching, they may make an arrest in order to discredit that witness's testimony.

After an arrest has taken place, it may be difficult to find the defendant. One way is to go to the police station and ask to see the log book on who was arrested at that time and place. Although those records are supposed to be public, they may refuse your request. Another way is to go to court and sit through the next arraignment session, or, to save time, just tell the Legal Aid Society or Public Defender that you are a witness to an arrest that took place at a certain date, time and place, and he or she should look out for the case and call you when necessary. As a witness to an illegal search, you can help even more by getting the names and addresses of possible other witnesses.

SEARCHES OF AUTOMOBILES

When are the police permitted to search automobiles?

Fourth amendment protections against searches of automobiles and drivers have been drastically reduced by the Supreme Court in the past year. These recent cases have affected not only automobile related searches but, by analogy, other searches, and they portend further weakening of the Fourth Amendment in the future. The general rule regarding searches of automobiles is the same as for any search; i.e., it must be with a warrant, incident to a

27

lawful arrest (which must be supported by probable cause), or on consent. It is in the area of searches incident to lawful arrests that the Court has greatly expanded police powers.

Formerly an additional rule existed in this area of law: the search incident to the lawful arrest had to be limited to weapons, "fruits," or instruments of the crime which led to the arrest. In December, 1973 the Supreme Court overruled several previous cases and held that any time a person is taken into custody for any reason, a full search can follow. *U.S. v. Robinson*, (decided December 11, 1973, unreported at time of printing). In this case Mr. Robinson was arrested for driving while his license was revoked, an offense for which there are no fruits, but he was taken to the police station, a thorough search revealed fourteen capsules of heroin, and the Court held that the search was reasonable. An important aspect of this District of Columbia case is that local regulations authorized the police to take the suspect into custody rather than issue a summons. (A summons is an order directing the person summoned to appear in court at a later date to answer the charge.) However, in a companion case decided at the same time, a man was arrested in Florida for driving without his license with him and a full search revealed marijuana. Local law did not specify whether the police should or should not make an arrest in such circumstances, but it did not prohibit an arrest. The Supreme Court held that the search in that case was also reasonable under the Fourth Amendment.

Thus the question of whether a search is lawful following a traffic offense appears to depend upon local (often city or county rather than state) law. If the police are *permitted* under local law to make a custodial arrest rather than issue a summons, a full search can follow, and it appears that if there is no local law on the subject then the police can make a custodial arrest. Unfortunately these decisions came too late for the preparation of a table of local laws. What will probably happen in practice is that when the police stop people for traffic offenses they will search them and if no contraband is found they will issue a summons, but if contraband is found they will claim that they made a lawful custodial arrest (if local regulations do not require the issuance of a summons) and the search was therefore lawful as being incident to the arrest. These decisions will also encourage the police to find the most minor violations (e.g. burned-out license plate light) in order to justify searches.

Searches that follow nontraffic arrests are covered by varying rules of law, depending on the circumstances, and there are differing rules emanating from different states. Generally speaking, if a nontraffic arrest takes place while the defendant is in a car, a short delay in searching the car is permissible. Where the arrest takes place outside the car, but the car is nearby, there is a difference of opinion about whether the search of the car is lawful. In *Conti v. Morgenthau,* 232 F. Supp. 1004 (1964), the Federal District Court in New York held that a search of the defendant's car, which was locked and parked around the corner from the defendant's apartment, was not incident to the arrest. But in *U.S. v. Baratta,* 397 F. 2d 215 (1968), the Federal Court of Appeals ruled that a warrantless search of the arrestee's car, when it was parked in the driveway of the house in which he was arrested, was lawful.

When a person is arrested in a car and taken to the police station, and the car is then searched, the rules also vary and depend, some courts have said, on the reasonableness of the later search in the light of all the circumstances surrounding the arrest and search. A search of locked trucks which were parked on the side of the highway after the defendants were removed from them and taken to jail was ruled illegal. (*McArthur v. Pennington*, 253 F. Supp. 420 [D.C. Tenn. 1963].) On the other hand, where the defendant was arrested on a highway and charged with counterfeiting, a search of the car later, at the police station, was found to be reasonable since the highway was crowded and it would have been dangerous to search the car there. The lawfulness of a later search may depend in part on the degree of seriousness of the crime for which the arrest was made.

In *Preston v. U.S.*, 376 U.S. 364 (1964), the Supreme Court ruled that where a man was arrested for vagrancy while in a car and the car was taken to the police station, and then towed to a police garage, a search of the car while it was in storage was illegal. However, many lower courts have upheld such searches, either on the ground that the car is lawfully in police custody (*Vaccaro v. U.S.*, 296 F. 2d 500 [C.A. Tex. 1961]) or on the ground that a search is justified as an inventory to protect the police from liability in case property is lost. This latter ruling was made by, among others, the Court of Appeals of New York in a case in which a car was searched after being towed away from a no-parking zone; the driver was arrested when he came to reclaim his car. (*People v. Sullivan*, 29 N.Y. 2d 69 [1971].) The Court of Appeals for the District of Columbia made an interesting ruling in the case of *Mayfield v. U.S.*, C.A.D.C. 4/15/71: contraband found in a car which was lawfully impounded after a traffic offender's arrest would not be admissible evidence of crime since the inventory was taken to protect the police from liability. This ruling is contrary to the thinking in almost all other jurisdictions where the general rule regards as admissible evidence anything found in the course of a lawful search notwithstanding the reason for the search.

What is the usual police practice with regard to searches of cars?

The police frequently stop cars in which minority-group people and youths are riding and simply order the occupants out of the car and search the people and the car. Usually the search is not very thorough, but it includes the glove compartment, the area under the front seat, the ashtrays, the trunk and often a cursory look through luggage. It almost never includes taking off door panels, looking inside a spare tire or taking apart anything that is securely fastened such as a rear seat or dashboard panel.

If contraband is found and an arrest made, the police testimony that follows an illegal search of a car is usually as follows: the officer says that he stopped the car to make a routine check of license and registration (which is legal everywhere and need not be supported by any probable cause) and then he saw the contraband in plain view, perhaps on the floor or on a seat.

How should you respond if the police search your car?

The same advice applies for searches of cars as for searches of persons: politely refuse to submit, but don't obstruct the police officer and don't be insistent about the fact that he is doing something illegal; try not to expose more people to arrest; look for witnesses; retrieve wrappings.

If contraband is found in a car, are all the occupants of the car automatically guilty of possession of the contraband?

Not necessarily. Most states still require the prosecution to prove that the possession was knowing, i.e., that the defendant knew it was there and knew what it was and that the particular defendant possessed the contraband. Where there are several passengers this may be difficult for the state to prove; where, for example, drugs are found in the trunk in a hidden place (not in one person's luggage) the state will have difficulty proving that the passengers possessed it. However, in New York a statute creates a presumption that if narcotics or weapons are found in a vehicle, they are presumed to belong to all occupants; in New Jersey the same presumption exists for weapons only. However, this is only a presumption and is rebuttable by evidence. If the contraband is found on one person, it is likely that, although all passengers might be arrested, only the actual possessor would be convicted.

SEARCHES OF HOMES

When can the police search homes?

Searches of homes are usually accomplished with search warrants. The legality of the search depends on whether the search warrant was lawfully issued by the judge who signed it, and on whether it was lawfully executed by the police.

How do the police get search warrants?

A police officer prepares the warrant (perhaps with the help of an assistant district attorney) which is a court order directing the police to search certain premises. He also prepares an affidavit in support of the warrant. Both are taken to a judge, and the officer appears before the judge. The judge must read and evaluate the affidavit to make sure it contains enough information so that there is probable cause to believe that a search of the designated premises will turn up contraband or evidence of a crime. If the judge has some doubts, he can question the police officer, under oath. Generally, the judge simply signs the warrant without closely examining the affidavit. For this reason, in most states, when there is a hearing after the arrest on a motion to quash a search warrant, the question of whether the warrant shows probable cause, and whether the statements contained in the warrant are true, is examined as though a decision on these questions had not previously been made.

33

What do the police have to show in order to get a warrant?

The affidavit in support of the warrant must show probable cause. A body of law has developed on what constitutes probable cause. In the majority of cases the information comes from an informer, who is, in drug cases, often an addict buying both drugs and his freedom by being an informer. The rule is that the informer's name need not be disclosed in the affidavit, but some basis must be given either for believing that the informer is reliable or corroborating the informer's story. Thus the affidavit may say in it that the informer proved reliable in two other cases, without naming them, or that the police officer corroborated the informer's story by watching the building and that he saw, for example, known addicts entering and leaving the premises. A recent Supreme Court case made it easier for the police to get search warrants by allowing the court to consider the police officer's statements on the defendant's reputation as a criminal; previously such statements were not entitled to any weight. (*U.S. v. Harris,* 91 S. Ct. 2075 [1971].)

Warrants must also be executed properly. Many states and the federal government now have "no-knock" laws on the books. This means that if the police can show in their affidavit that the evidence being sought (usually drugs) can be quickly disposed of, the judge can provide in the warrant that the police can enter a home without knocking, i.e., they can just break the door in. If the police break in without a no-knock order, the evidence should be supressible on the grounds that the warrant was not lawfully executed. Some states also have laws limiting the time

34

during which warrants can be executed to daylight hours, or, as in New York, to between 6:00 A.M. and 9:00 P.M., unless the warrant authorizes night-time entry. Another frequent requirement is that the information contained in the affidavit must not be stale; what constitutes staleness is nowhere specifically defined but depends on the totality of circumstances. Most warrants must be executed within a specified short time, depending on state law, of perhaps ten days, and the warrant becomes void at the expiration of that time. These requirements become important later on when a motion is made, and a hearing is held on the motion, to quash the search warrant and suppress the evidence (see Chapter III).

What about searches conducted without a warrant?

Because the procedure for getting warrants is cumbersome, and because warrants are often quashed, the police often search without warrants. They use several different tactics. If there is a party going on, they may come to the door on the pretext that there has been a complaint about noise; when the door is opened, they enter, search and arrest. At the hearing on the motion to suppress, they testify that when the door was opened, they saw drugs plainly in view, which gave them probable cause to arrest and then search. Another tactic is to use an informer to knock on the door, and when the door is opened the police come out of their hiding places, barge in and search. They then allege that they saw the sale of drugs take place between the occupants of the house and the informer, they arrest both (the informer is charged with possession), and the informer is freed by the court when the judge is told that he is an informer. Another way the police gain entrance sometimes occurs in a situation when someone has shipped drugs, usually marijuana or hashish, by mail or parcel post. The police and post office now have dogs that can smell the contraband even when it is concealed inside something else: they conceal themselves when the postman delivers the package, and once it is delivered they arrest the recipient and search the house. Since they have probable cause for arrest at the time they enter, such cases are difficult to defend on the grounds that the search of the house was illegal. Fortunately, some of these cases have been won on the grounds that if the police opened the package in the post office after the dog sniffed it out they must have a search warrant, which they usually do not get. The police have gotten around this in some cases by claiming that the package fell to the ground and opened accidentally, and some judges have condoned this obvious lie. A few other cases of this type have been dismissed for another reason: the sender dispatched the package to a third person, perhaps nonexistent, in care of the actual recipient. Since the arrest took place immediately after the package was delivered, the recipient maintained that the real addressee was away, and that he or she had no knowledge of what was in the package.

When an arrest takes place in a home, the police cannot lawfully conduct a search of the entire house or apartment as a search incident to the arrest, although they often do just that. In the case of *Chimel v. California*, 395 U.S. 752 (1969), the Supreme Court held that such searches had to be limited to the person arrested and the area into which the arrestee might reach in order to grab weapons or evidentiary items. This probably means the same room, although it is not clear exactly what area can be searched. Police have been able to ignore this ruling by simply testifying that whatever contraband or evidence they found was in the vicinity of the defendant.

As with most other illegal searches, the problem is most often an evidentiary one. If the police break in your door without a warrant, which does happen, you should take photographs of the door and have it looked at by an impartial third person as soon after the incident as possible and before it is repaired. If your home is ransacked by the police, take photographs of this also. Use common sense in gathering evidence and seek the aid of a lawyer as soon as possible.

Should the police knock on your door, remember that you are under no legal obligation to open it unless they have a warrant. If they say they want to talk to you, you are under no obligation to talk to them or, if you prefer, you can tell them that you will talk to them through the closed door. If they claim to have a warrant, ask them to hold it up to the peephole or slip it under the door. After seeing the warrant, you can still refuse to open the door, but the police will then break it down.

It is important to note that the existence of contraband in an apartment or house does not in itself create any presumptions that the occupants of the premises possessed the contraband. For example, if several people were living in a house or apartment and contraband was found in a common area, say the kitchen or bathroom, and neither of those areas was the exclusive domain of any person on the premises, very likely none of the occupants of the premises could be convicted of possession of the contraband, although everyone would probably be arrested. Only the state of Maine has a statute making it a crime to knowingly be on premises where cannabis or peyote is kept, or to knowingly be in the company of a person possessing it. Of course, many other factors *can* lead to conviction, such as the contraband being found in a suitcase belonging to a particular person or in a room occupied by a particular person.

BORDER AND AIRPLANE SEARCHES

What are the limits of border and airplane searches, and what is the nature of them?

Federal law gives customs officials the authority to detain and search anyone or anything coming in from a foreign country, including Canada and Mexico. However, the Fourth Amendment requirement that all searches be "reasonable" also applies to border searches. Courts have held that such searches are reasonable even if made on the basis of mere suspicion, which can be anything from an informer's tip to the behavior of the person crossing the border. Warrants are not required.

Searches that go as far as looking into body cavities, however, must be based on more than mere suspicion; there must be a "clear indication" or "plain suggestion" of criminal activity. In the case of *Rivas v. U.S.*, 368 F. 2d 703 (1966), a previously convicted and registered narcotics user came across a border in an obviously high condition and the court held that a rectal search resulting in drugs being found was lawful. On the other hand, where a customs official erroneously thought he recognized a woman who was crossing the border as a previously arrested smuggler, a search of her vagina was held to have been based on—at most—mere suspicion, and the evidence found was suppressed as illegally seized. (*Henderson v. U.S.*, 390 F. 2d 805 [1966].)

A less thorough search of luggage, clothing being worn, packages or a vehicle will in practice always be found lawful. Much of this searching is done to apprehend smugglers of goods as well as to find drugs. Naturally, young people and minority-group people are more prone to being searched than older and conventional-looking white people. Most border searches at piers and airports consist of perfunctory examinations of luggage and handbags; an occasional search will be more thorough. At the Canadian and Mexican borders, most cars pass through with nothing more than a guard looking into the car and, perhaps, looking into a handbag. Periodically, a car is ordered into a special line and a more thorough search made. Guards look for evidence of smuggling, such as panels that appear to have been removed, and if they find any they dismantle the car. Arrests at borders are almost certain to lead to convictions, and the prosecution takes place in federal court where the sentences are often severe.

Interstate airplane flights, where no national borders are crossed, are subject to a special search system. Prior to the hijacking era, and the subsequent antihijacking system devised by the government, interstate baggage could not be searched at all by government officials. Recently the government set forth rules for searches based upon a "crime-prone profile," which is supposedly based upon the characteristics of hijackers; under the rules, government inspection agents make a thorough search and check the identification of a certain percentage, or perhaps all—they will not say—of those fitting these preconceived traits. In addition, all passengers' carry-on luggage is opened and briefly looked into, and all passengers are required to walk through a gun-detecting device called a magnetometer, which also detects other metal objects. Persons registering positively on the machine are searched. The airlines will not disclose the details of their system, supposedly to prevent prospective hijackers from changing their appearance for a hijacking, but it seems certain that the crime-prone profile includes traits of minority groups and long-haired types.

Are persons other than hijacking suspects arrested in these searches?

Yes. During a twenty-two-month period ending December 1972, almost six thousand people were arrested at airports. Less than twenty percent of these arrests were for carrying a gun, threatening to hijack, or for other charges relating to hijacking. Over two thousand people were arrested for possession of drugs, and about the same number were arrested for illegal entry. Others were arrested on charges ranging from parole violation to forgery.* The

*New York Times, 11/26/72, page 1, column 1.

nature of these arrests makes it clear that the searches and questioning that take place go much further than necessary to find potential hijackers.

Are such searches constitutional?

As of February 1973, this question had not been decided. The American Civil Liberties Union takes the position that such searches are unconstitutional; the Justice Department believes the opposite. Several lower courts have upheld the system, but the system has changed several times and the Supreme Court has not yet ruled. One federal district court held that where an airline went further and added other criteria to the crime-prone profile, the delicate balance upon which the constitutionality of the system rests was upset and the search was unconstitutional. (*U.S. v. Lopez*, E.D.N.Y. 5/7/71.) Another federal court held that the results of airport searches would not be admissible unless the passenger was told that he could refuse to be searched, in which case he would not be allowed on the plane.*

LOITERING AND VAGRANCY

Loitering and vagrancy laws are one of the most common sources of the harassment that youths and minority groups face—the order to move on, when one is just "hanging" around, the request for identification, and ques-

New York Times, 12/10/72.

tions about what one is doing and where one is going
when he or she is just walking the streets. Police seem not
to understand why people are ever on the streets at night.
When I was thirteen, I saw a very moving theatrical play
and took a walk to think about it. A policeman stopped
me and asked what I was doing. I replied that I was
walking. He asked where to. I answered nowhere and he
asked what I was doing. I again said walking and he said
but what are you doing? I replied that I was thinking, and
he then asked me if I had ever been in a mental institu-
tion.

**Are the state loitering and vagrancy statutes constitu-
tional?**

Several such statutes have been declared unconstitutional in the last few years on the grounds either that they are
too vague in defining a crime, or that they prohibit conduct which the state has no right to prohibit. Recently the
Supreme Court in the case of *Papachristou v. Jacksonville*,
405 U.S. 156 (1972), invalidated a Jacksonville ordinance
that outlawed vagrants, who were defined as "rogues and
vagabonds, or dissolute persons who go about begging,
. . . common night walkers, . . . persons strolling from
place to place without any lawful purpose, habitual loaf-
ers, . . . persons able to work but habitually living upon
the earnings of their wives. . . ." In an exceptionally en-
lightened and strong opinion, the Court said that the
statute was unconstitutional because it was vague (it did
not give the average citizen notice of what was illegal);
overbroad (it included obviously lawful conduct such as

strolling and living off the earnings of a wife); it encouraged arbitrary and erratic arrests; and it placed too much discretion in the hands of the police. Although this decision only nullifies Jacksonville's ordinance, the language in it is the law of the land and should influence other rulings on state and local laws in the future.

There have also been state court decisions on vagrancy laws. In Maine a statute which made it a crime to be an "idle and disorderly person(s), having no visible means of support, neglecting all lawful calling or employment" was thrown out. (*Knowlton v. State of Maine,* 257 A. 2d 409 [1969].) In Massachusetts there was a statute empowering the police "during the nighttime . . . to examine persons abroad whom they have reason to suspect of unlawful design, and to demand of them their business, and whither they are going, and to arrest and prosecute persons so suspected who fail to give a satisfactory account of themselves." The highest court in the state held the statute unconstitutional insofar as it attempts to define a substantive violation of law, but valid insofar as it permits a "brief threshold of inquiry." (*Alegata v. Commonwealth,* 231 N.E. 2d 201 [1967].) In the case of *Hayes v. Municipal Court,* Okla. Ct. Crim. App., 7/28/71, a statute prohibiting "loitering and wandering without a lawful reason for being at such a place at such time" was held unconstitutionally vague and overbroad. In this case, a curfew banning youths under sixteen from loafing or loitering on streets between 9:00 P.M. and 6:00 A.M. was also invalidated on the grounds that it unlawfully discriminated against youths.

In another Supreme Court case on this subject, *Coates*

v. Cincinnati, 91 S. Ct. 1686 (1971), the Court invalidated a statute which made it "unlawful for 3 or more persons to assemble . . . in a manner annoying to persons passing by." The ground for the decision was primarily that people could not know what is annoying to passers-by, and that the government cannot ban all conduct that is annoying to passers-by.

However, these decisions apply only to the particular state statutes ruled upon and the unconstitutional statute may be rewritten, perhaps also vaguely or too broadly, soon after the court decision. Testing each state's statute is difficult since the cases are either dismissed or the penalties are so small that people would often rather pay a fine and leave. Furthermore, the decisions have never directly confronted the issues of whether the police can lawfully prevent people from hanging out at particular places; it seems that courts have not wanted to prevent the police from telling people who are hanging out to move on. In New York, when a great number of arrests for loitering for the purpose of using narcotics resulted in dismissal, the district attorney and police commissioner had to direct patrolmen not to invoke this law for purposes of harassment, but only upon clear proof that narcotics were about to be used.

When the cop on the beat tells you to move on, or stops you to ask for identification and where you are going, your failure to move on or answer will almost surely lead to an arrest. You may spend the night in jail, and the next day the case may be dismissed or you will be allowed to plead guilty to some minor charge and be sentenced to time served or a small fine. That doesn't

44

change the fact that you cannot hang out when and where you want to. In this area, perhaps more than any other, a lawsuit may be a viable way to change things, at least temporarily. The language in many of the statutes sounds as if it comes from seventeenth-century England, and many courts may be ready to invalidate them.

SHOPLIFTING LAWS

Are store personnel allowed to search suspected shoplifters?

Thirty states have laws which allow merchants and their employees to stop people whom they suspect of shoplifting and hold them for the police. The laws vary from state to state, some permitting detention, others allowing questioning and some authorizing searches (see Table 2). There have been few cases on the legality of these statutes, although it seems clear that in view of the great amount of shoplifting that takes place in this country, almost all courts would uphold these laws.

For those states without laws covering the powers of merchants, the general law regarding citizens' arrests would apply. These laws usually provide that citizens can make arrests by forcibly bringing someone to a police station or holding them for the police. The result of this situation is that, with the few limitations shown in the table, merchants and their employees are within the law in forcibly detaining someone for the police.

Table 2
Synopsis of Laws Regarding Detention of Alleged Shoplifters by Merchants

Alabama	reasonable detention
Arkansas	reasonable detention (No liability if wrong.)
Colorado	reasonable questioning
Florida	reasonable detention in order to obtain return of goods
Georgia	reasonable detention
Illinois	reasonable detention
Indiana	1 hour limit on detention (no longer than 1 hour on arrival of peace officer)
Iowa	no search without permission of accused unless the searcher is acting under the direction of a peace officer
Kansas	reasonable detention
Kentucky	reasonable detention
Louisiana	may question for 60 minutes and use reasonable force to detain
Massachusetts	reasonable detention
Michigan	reasonable detention
Minnesota	detention only for purpose of delivering suspect to police; no interrogation against the suspect's will
Missouri	reasonable detention
Nebraska	reasonable detention
New Jersey	reasonable detention
New Mexico	reasonable detention
New York	reasonable detention
North Carolina	reasonable detention
Oklahoma	reasonable detention
Rhode Island	reasonable detention
South Dakota	detention until police arrive

46

Tennessee	detention for purpose of recovering goods (search)
Utah	detention for purpose of recovering goods (search)
Washington	detention for purpose of recovering goods (search)
West Virginia	detention for no longer than 30 minutes
Wisconsin	reasonable detention to deliver suspect to police; suspect can make phone calls while being so detained by merchant and suspect cannot be interrogated or searched without his consent.
Wyoming	reasonable detention

II

Rights Upon Arrest

From the time that a person is told that he or she is under arrest until the time that he or she is brought before a judge, that person is physically under the complete control of the police department and there is little that can be done about it. During that time a person has some rights, but very few and little power to enforce them. The source of those rights are some Supreme Court decisions, state statutes, and local police department regulations, which vary greatly. The biggest problem in this area is that there is really no way to enforce these rights. The police will obey most of them most of the time, except when it suits them not to. With the exception of the warnings on confessions, and the right to counsel at lineups, there are virtually no penalties imposed against the police for disobeying any of the rules and violating the rights of a person arrested.

PHONE CALLS, PERSONAL PROPERTY, BEING INFORMED OF CHARGES

What is the general procedure that immediately follows an arrest?

After a person is arrested, he or she is brought to a police station, booked (i.e., forms are filled out about the arrest, the arrestee's background, occupation, etc.), fingerprinted, and sometimes, depending on the state and the charges, photographed. Many police departments have regulations giving arrestees the right to make a certain number of phone calls to a lawyer and a family member or friend, and providing for the care of personal property in the possession of the arrestee. In most instances these regulations are obeyed, but in many cases, where the police are hostile to the arrestee, they do not allow a phone call or feed the person or allow him to keep the personal property he is entitled to. The post-arrest regulations in fifteen cities that responded to our questionnaire are contained in Table 3.

Table 3
Some Local Post-Arrest Regulations

City	Regulations
Baltimore	2 phone calls; only unlawful or dangerous property, evidence and valuables removed one call; all personal property taken
Chicago	reasonable number of phone calls; no property rules
Cincinnati	phone calls can be made before being assigned to a cell; 3 calls every 24 hours

	allowed. Only have regulations concerning confiscation of unlawfully held property
Dallas	No particular limit on calls; only valuables and items which could aid escape are taken
Detroit	arrestee can phone attorney and friend or relative; all personal property taken
Honolulu	phone calls permitted, all personal property except glasses and handkerchief removed
Indianapolis	one phone call; all personal property removed
Nashville	right to one completed call before being booked but after 1 hour arrestee can be booked without having completed call
Philadelphia	one completed phone call and jail sergeant can allow more; all personal property including belts and shoelaces and sometimes shoes are taken
Phoenix	phone calls to communicate with attorney, family, or friends; all personal property taken

Do the police have to inform arrestees of the charges against them at the time of the arrest?

Yes, although in fact, some people do not even know that they have been arrested until some time after they arrive at the police station; the police, to avoid trouble, often simply tell people that they want to talk to them in the police station, and the people go along and are told later that they have been arrested. Virtually no one is informed of the charges until some time after they arrive at the precinct, and sometimes not until they get to court. The few regulations on this subject provide that people must be informed of the charges in the precinct. There is

53

no way to enforce such rules without a lawyer in the precinct, and of course the matter is moot by the time the case gets to court and a complaint is drawn up. Also, the initial statement of charges by the police officer is not binding, since in most places it is the district attorney who decides exactly what the charges will be.

CONFESSIONS

Can the police legally question arrestees in order to try to obtain a confession to use at trial?

Yes. However, a confession, or any statement, in order to be admissible in a trial, must be voluntarily given and the police must first have given certain warnings, called *Miranda* warnings, to the defendant before questioning him or her. The *Miranda* warnings, so called because they are derived from the case of *Miranda v. Arizona,* 384 U.S. 436 (1966) are: (1) you have a right to remain silent; (2) anything you say can be used as evidence against you in a trial; (3) you have a right to a lawyer; and (4) if you want a lawyer and cannot afford one, a lawyer will be appointed without cost to you. It is also required that the police give these warnings in such a manner that the person arrested understands them. If the defendant asks for a lawyer or does not want to answer questions, the questioning must stop.

Do the police have to give the Miranda warnings to all persons who have been arrested?

No. They must give the warnings only to those persons whom they want to question.

Unlike the situation with many other post-arrest, pre-court rights, there is a sanction against the police if they fail to give the warnings: any confession taken in violation of them will not be admissible in evidence. However, it is the experience of many legal workers that the police often do not give the *Miranda* warnings prior to questioning. Interrogation usually takes place in an empty room in a police station shortly after arrest before there is a lawyer on the scene; if the police are able to obtain a confession, they simply testify at the hearing on the motion to suppress the confession that they gave the required warnings. Such a hearing boils down to a swearing contest between the police and the defendant—there are almost never any nonpolice witnesses to the interrogation—and most judges, in deciding whether the confession was lawfully obtained, assume it was.

If the Miranda warnings have been properly given, are all confessions made after the warnings admissible in evidence?

No. For a confession to be admissible, it must also be voluntary under another body of case law that preceded *Miranda*. Brutality, or threats of brutality, make a confession involuntary, but the misconduct need not go that far. Frightening, undressing, denying food or medicine, promising leniency, using a friend or relative, or using a psychological trick (such as telling the defendant that his partner confessed and implicated him), can also, depending partly on the court, invalidate a confession. Physical or mental infirmities that reduce the will to resist may become factors in determining voluntariness. The length of the questioning may also be important. For more detail on this, see *Law and Tactics in Exclusionary Hearings* by Thomas P. Abbott and others (Coiner Publishing, Washington, D.C.), Chapter 8.

What should a citizen do when being questioned by the police?

Virtually every lawyer will agree that the best advice to someone being questioned by the police is to say absolutely nothing other than your name and address. It is not easy for the average citizen to resist giving some kind of statement. The police are sometimes skilled interrogators; many have learned techniques for "opening people up." Sometimes they play the good guy–bad guy game, in which one policeman acts threatening and violent and the other acts as though he is trying to protect the defendant from his rough partner; one threatens punishment and the other promises rewards and in that way the defendant becomes frightened and also starts to trust the "good guy." As a general rule, one should never believe a promise made by a policeman, nor should one believe a threat. Another common police technique is to pursue any minor statement the defendant makes, ask him to explain it and then try to use it as a wedge to get him to say more. They may also insist that a defendant's partner confessed or relate

56

some misinformation they have so that you will contradict it. In spite of how difficult it is for the defendant to resist making some kind of statement the most seemingly harmless of which may be damaging at trial, the best thing to do is to say absolutely nothing. This means that to every question that is asked, you should answer that you have nothing to say. Remember that once you are being interrogated, and the police have some evidence against you, you will not be able to talk yourself out of an arrest no matter what you say. Even if you are innocent, and perhaps have an ironclad alibi, you are better off disclosing the information at a later time, after you or your lawyer have been able to check it out and make sure your witness remembers. Remember, too, that your refusal to answer any questions cannot be held against you in any way later on, but a slightly mistaken or inaccurate statement can be used against you at trial.

What if you are approached by the police and told that they want to talk to you at the police station?

In conducting an investigation, the police often pick people up, bring them to the police station and question them. They do not have enough evidence for an arrest, but they ask the person to come along to the police station, and if the person refuses they may force her. Questioning at this state has been called "custodial interrogation"; the citizen is in a state of custody that is less than arrest. Except for the situation covered by the Uniform Arrest Act, discussed on page 19, forcing a person to remain in such custody is probably illegal, although the Supreme Court has not yet ruled on this subject. If the police fail to give the *Miranda* warnings, any statements made during such custody would, of course, be inadmissible in court. Several courts, but not the Supreme Court, have held, however, that if the *Miranda* warnings are given, statements made during custodial interrogation are admissible. These rulings seem to contradict earlier Supreme Court rulings which held, in effect, that any evidence obtained as a result of illegal police activity is inadmissible. The illegal activity here would be simply keeping a person in custody without probable cause to arrest. The law in this area is still developing, but most courts lean toward admitting confessions.

At the point of asking you to go with them, the police will usually act very friendly and say that they just want to discuss some matters with you; don't be misled into assuming that they want to talk to you as a friend. Even in states which have the Uniform Arrest Act, covering another type of circumstance, it seems probable that, unless there is an actual arrest, the citizen has the right to refuse. You can ask if you are under arrest, and if they say no you can tell them politely that you refuse to accompany them and that, if they order or force you to go with them, this means that they have arrested you and according to the Fourth Amendment to the United States Constitution, they cannot arrest you unless they have probable cause. If they then insist you must, of course, obey unless you want to risk being forced and/or beaten. At the police station, you can again ask if you are under arrest and if you are not, you should say that you are leaving and begin to walk out the door. If the police do not let you leave, you should insist on having a lawyer and if you cannot afford one, you can tell them that they have the responsibility to get you a lawyer free of charge. You should refuse to answer any questions; this may result in your release since, if they did not arrest you in the first place, it means that they might not have sufficient evidence to hold you.

The Supreme Court has held that the police do not have the right to round up people against whom they have no evidence and take the fingerprints of those people. See *Davis v. Mississippi, supra,* discussed on page 19. Should you be picked up, not formally arrested and directed to submit to fingerprinting, you have the right to refuse; the police will be unable to take your fingerprints against your will since the slightest movement will spoil the print.

LINEUPS

How are identifications of suspects made by complaining witnesses?

There are two different kinds of identification procedures: "showups," in which the victim simply views the suspect by himself, either in the police precinct or wherever he happens to be, and "lineups," in which the suspect is placed among a group of persons who have somewhat similar physical characteristics, and the victim is asked to identify him. Often showups and lineups are conducted before the suspect has been formally arrested.

Can the police force someone whom they have not yet arrested to participate in a lineup?

Although it is not yet decided, it appears that, following the reasoning of the Supreme Court in *Davis v. Mississippi*, the police do not have the right to detain persons against whom they have no evidence for the purpose of having those persons participate in a lineup. Should you be asked to participate in a lineup, without having been formally arrested, you have the right to refuse and you may be able to physically resist participating in the lineup by turning around or covering your face.

Does a person have the right to have a lawyer present at a lineup or showup that takes place before a formal arrest has been made?

No. The Supreme Court held in the case of *Kirby v. Illinois*, 406 U.S. 682 (1972), that there was no right to a lawyer at a lineup where the defendants were not yet formally charged. The court noted, however, that the defendants did not ask for legal assistance, although even if they had requested counsel the decision by the present Supreme Court would probably have been the same. This does not mean that a person who is asked to be in a lineup should not ask for a lawyer—he should. It is possible that the police will grant the request and furnish a lawyer, or that they will give the arrestee's own lawyer a chance to get there before the lineup. A lawyer can be helpful at a lineup by making sure that the lineup or showup is not conducted in a way that leads the complaining witness or in any other way influences identification.

Does a person have the right to have a lawyer present at a lineup conducted after he has been indicted?

Yes. The Supreme Court so held in the case of *U.S. v. Wade*, 388 U.S. 218 (1967), and the present Supreme Court, in deciding *Kirby*, did not specifically overrule *Wade*; its decision in *Kirby* simply limited the right to counsel to lineups taking place after charges have been brought. If a lineup takes place after indictment, and no lawyer is present and the defendant has not waived his right to counsel, then the witness will not be able to testify at trial that he or she identified the defendant at that lineup.

Is it required that lineups and showups not be conducted in a suggestive manner?

Yes. The Supreme Court so held in the case of *Stovall v. Denno*, 388 U.S. 293 (1967). However, it is probable that most lineups are suggestive nevertheless, since the standins are usually police officers and can readily be distinguished from the suspect in the lineup. Although the overall physical characteristics such as height, weight, etc., may be similar, it seems obvious that police officers have a neater appearance, a different facial expression, and a different posture than people who have been in prison, or who use drugs, or who simply have been in the ghetto all their lives. Unfortunately, the courts have not taken this position.

Have showups been held by the courts to be per se suggestive and, therefore, illegal?

No. In a recent Supreme Court case it was stated that showups are not per se illegal, although they cannot be conducted in a suggestive manner. There have been some cases in which showup identifications were held to be unfairly suggestive and inadmissible, such as where the suspect is handcuffed and pushed around by the police in the presence of the complaining witness.

If a judge finds at a hearing that the identification procedure conducted after the crime was illegal or unfairly suggestive, this does not necessarily mean that the case is thrown out. If the judge finds that the victim had a substantial opportunity to view the defendant at the time of the crime, then, although the evidence of the early identification procedure is excluded, the court will permit the witness to testify during the trial that the defendant was the one who committed the crime. This is called an in-court identification. However, if the contact between the victim and assailant was very brief, the court may find that the bad identification procedure tainted all later identification procedures, and therefore an in-court identification will not be permitted. This usually results in the case being dismissed, since in most cases there is no evidence other than the identification by the victim. Therefore, such rulings are rare.

THE RIGHT TO BE RELEASED FROM THE POLICE STATION

What are the conditions for release following arrest?

The rules regarding release from the police station vary from state to state and are covered in general in Table 4. For example, in New York the police-department regulations prescribe that in certain crimes (non felonies) the arresting officer is to conduct an interview pursuant to a form, on subjects indicating roots in the community, such as the number of years the person has lived at his particular address, the number of years the person has lived in the community, family ties, employment, schooling and prior criminal record. Verification by a friend or relative, either by telephone or in person, is also required. If the interviewee achieves a certain number of points as set forth by a formula, she is released from the police station on a summons, without bail. However, the law also prescribes that the arresting officer can refuse to issue a summons if, in his discretion, he feels that it may lead to further disorders in the community, which means in practice that the police officer can refuse to issue a summons

Table 4
States in Which Arrestees can be Released From
*Police Station**

	With Bail	Without Bail
Alabama	X (M)†	
California		X (M)
Connecticut	X	X
Delaware		X (M)
Georgia	X (M)	

63

Indiana	X	(if amount indicated on warrant)	
Hawaii	X	(for crimes punishable by less than 2 years)	
Louisiana	X	(violation of municipal ordinances)	
Missouri	X (M)		
Montana	X (M)	(if justice of peace or police judge has posted schedule of cash bail)	
Nevada	X (M)		
New Hampshire			X (M)
New Jersey	X (M)		
New Mexico	where a warrant is issued for arrest, judge *must* indicate on it the amount of bail and authorize officer to accept it		
New York	X (M)		X (M)
Ohio	X	(M, when judge not available and in accord with posted schedule)	
Oklahoma			X (only for violation of fish, game and water safety laws)
Pennsylvania	X (M)		
Texas	X (M)	(F, when court is not in session in the county where defendant is in custody)	
Virginia	X (M)		
Wyoming	X (M)		

*Note: For the states not listed, the arrestee cannot be released from the police station.
†M=Misdemeanors only.

when he is angry. The law also provides that the arrestee can be required to post bail, in the discretion of the arresting officer, of up to five hundred dollars for misdemeanors. This is called stationhouse bail. The discretionary power to refuse to issue a summons, or to require bail, is frequently abused by the police. The only remedy for an abuse of discretion is to try to get a lawyer to the police station and urge him to make complaints to superiors in the police department.

Some special rules exist if the person arrested is a juvenile. The age at which one stops being treated as a juvenile varies from state to state and is set forth in Table 5. In most states the police must release juveniles to the custody of a parent or guardian, pending arraignment at a later date, except for the most serious cases such as homicide, when the juvenile can be held.

Table 5
Age at Which Persons Are No Longer Treated as Juveniles

Alabama	16–18
Alaska	18
Arizona	18
Arkansas	18
California	18–21
Colorado	16, if punishable by death or life imprisonment, otherwise 18
Connecticut	16–18
Delaware	18
District of Columbia	18
Florida	17
Georgia	17
Hawaii	18
Idaho	18
Illinois	17–boys, 18–girls

Indiana	18
Iowa	18
Kansas	18
Kentucky	18
Louisiana	17–21
Maine	17
Maryland	16–18
Massachusetts	14–17
Michigan	17
Minnesota	18
Mississippi	18
Missouri	17
Montana	18
Nebraska	16–18
Nevada	18
New Hampshire	17
New Jersey	varies from 16–18
New Mexico	18
New York	16–18 for girls "in need of supervision; 18 for boys"
North Carolina	16
North Dakota	14–18
Ohio	18
Oklahoma	18–girls, 16–boys, except Tulsa where it is 18 for both
Oregon	18
Pennsylvania	16–18
Rhode Island	16–18
South Carolina	16–18, varies by county
South Dakota	18
Tennessee	varies from 16 to 18, generally 17
Texas	10–17, boys; 18, girls
Utah	18
Vermont	16
Virginia	varies from 18 to 21
Washington	18
West Virginia	16–18
Wisconsin	16–18
Wyoming	18–19, boys; 18–21, girls

Criminal law is a very specialized field. The case law, the procedures both in and out of court, the jargon—all are peculiar to criminal law. Perhaps most important, there is an atmosphere of hostility which is much more pervasive in criminal than civil cases. In big cities, there is usually a small group of lawyers who practice only criminal law, while all others may do little or none. In small towns, what few lawyers there are do only a small amount of criminal law work as a sideline to civil law practice. In any event, none but the specialists know the finer tricks of the trade, and therefore, if you should ever be arrested, you should know what you have the right to expect from the lawyer you call to the local precinct.

What should a lawyer do at the police station?
First of all, every lawyer should tell an arrestee to make no statements other than name, address, and personal data such as employment or occupation, family, etc. Where an arrestee is being interviewed for release on a summons, the detailed questions on background are usually not damaging admissions and should be answered. The police will always ask for the particulars of any previous arrests on your part. If an arrestee refuses to be finger-printed or photographed after an arrest, the result will almost certainly be a very high bail or no bail at all since the judge will assume that the arrestee is trying to conceal her identity.

The lawyer's basic function in the police station is to begin preparation for representing his or her client in court. The first court proceeding after arrest is the arraignment, which is a very brief proceeding in which the defendant is informed of the charges against him (unless he waives the reading of the charges, which all lawyers will do since they can simply read the written complaint), and in which the judge sets a bail or releases the defendant without bail, after the defense lawyer makes a statement to the court about the defendant's background. The lawyer must therefore get from his client what are generally referred to as "bail facts." These are all the facts that show the arrestee's roots in the community and reliability, which, together with the seriousness of the alleged crime and the defendant's prior criminal record, are the only factors that the court can consider in setting bail. (*Stack v. Boyle*, 342 U.S. 1 [1951].) In a few states (notably New York) and in federal cases the law has sanctioned preventive detention in which bail can be denied if an arrestee has a long prior record and if there is a substantial amount of proof against him on the new charge. However, in all other states there is a right to bail and it is illegal for judges to set bail at an absurdly high amount, that they know the defendant cannot post, in order to make sure that the defendant stays in jail. The fact that it is illegal does not mean that it is uncommon; in fact it is the general practice in most states. The specific bail facts include such information as the number of years the person has resided in the community, the number of years he has resided at a particular address, his employment record, his educational background, his family ties and family responsibilities (i.e., how many dependents he has), whether the defendant lives with his parents, and any civic organizations he is a member of or participates in, including regular attendance at a community center or a Y.M.C.A. or Y.W.C.A.

It is also helpful to have as many people as possible appear in court on the defendant's behalf, such as parents, social workers, ministers, employers, friends, etc., and it is appropriate in most courts for them to stand up, either at the railing separating the judge's area from the spectators' area or at their seats, when the arguments are being heard in order to show their support for the defendant. This tactic may be helpful since the judge, on occasion, may respond to the fact that many people are concerned about this individual, and their concern indicates roots in the community and reliability. The presence of members of the public may also embarrass the judge into being more reasonable. Thus, at the police station, your lawyer should be getting names of people to bring to court on your behalf.

The lawyer should also be preparing to defend the case in its later stages. Information gotten at the police station can be very important at trial. For example, if the lawyer has a casual conversation with the arresting police officer, and the officer says that he gained possession of the evidence in a certain way, and if the police officer changes that story in court, the lawyer will be able to introduce into evidence the earlier statement in order to discredit the officer's testimony. Thus the defense lawyer should have a chat with the arresting officer in as friendly and casual a way as possible. If your lawyer does not talk to the police officer, you should tell him to. Although many police officers know that they have no obligation to talk to a defense lawyer, most will respond if the defense lawyer is skillful enough. If the police officer refuses to talk when first approached, it may prove successful to make several attempts, each time with a new question or statement, until he finally opens up. Or he may respond if the lawyer tells him what his client's version of the facts are, since he may want to defend himself against what he considers an unjust accusation.

Another important piece of information that the lawyer should get is the charge that the police officer initially lodges against the defendant. In case the charges are increased by the district attorney, the defense lawyer can sometimes impeach the police officer's version of the facts by pointing out that the police officer charged a lesser crime at the police station. Where there is contraband that has been seized, the lawyer should carefully examine it to make sure it is not switched before trial (occasionally pills are seized that are not illegal drugs, although the defendant may be selling them as illegal drugs, and the police sometimes replace the phony drugs with real drugs before trial). The lawyer should also be examining any wrappings of contraband to make sure that wrappings which might show an illegal search are not discarded before trial.

The lawyer can also be helpful in the pre-arraignment phase of the proceedings by calling people to help post bail, finding references where they are required for release on a summons, convincing police officers to issue a summons where they otherwise might not or making complaints to superiors in the police department where a police officer improperly refuses to write a summons. Such miscellaneous duties as getting food and cigarettes for the defendant if the police refuse to do so should not be considered beneath a lawyer's function. In certain cases, the lawyer who is willing to sit with his client for several hours until the arraignment may even prevent a beating from taking place. (And if you think beatings do not occur in police stations, you're wrong.)

MISCELLANEOUS QUESTIONS ABOUT WHAT GOES ON AT THE POLICE STATION

What questions asked by the police should a citizen answer after being arrested?

First, and most important, it should be repeated that an arrestee need not answer any questions at all; he is not even required to give his name. Furthermore, there is no law that says that an arrestee must be honest; the arrestee is not under oath and lying in the police station is not perjury. However, it is usually wise to give one's name and address (unless you fear a search of your house), because otherwise you may be held in jail after arraignment without bail on the grounds that if a person does not give his name it is clear he is likely not to return to court for trial.

There is nothing wrong with disclosing your place of employment, unless you fear being fired if your employer finds out that you have been arrested. Although it is not a regular police practice to inform employers of arrests, a particularly nasty police officer may do so on his own initiative. If you are being interviewed to determine eligibility for release on a summons, many more detailed questions will be asked such as whom you live with, length of time at your residence, names of references, etc. There is generally no harm in answering all these questions but if for some reason you do not wish to answer them, you can refuse to do so in which case, of course, a summons will not be issued. You will then have to wait until you get to court for the judge either to set bail or release you on your own recognizance.

III

Rights in Court

THE ARRAIGNMENT

What happens at the arraignment, and when does it take place?

As we mentioned in the last chapter, the arraignment is the first court proceeding after arrest, and in it the defendant is informed of the charges, bail facts are presented to the court by the defense attorney or the defendant, bail is set or the defendant is released without bail and the case is adjourned to another day. You should be arraigned within several hours of the arrest, or at most a day later. Some states have laws requiring the police to bring the arrestee before a judge within a certain specified period of time, as enumerated in Table 6; however, in most states the law says only that it must be done promptly or within a reasonable time. It seems safe to assume that "promptly" means within, at most, a day after the arrest. In large cities where the processing of cases is systematized and takes place almost continuously, including weekends, arraignments almost always take place within the required time. However, there are occasional

Table 6
*State Laws on Time Within Which Arrestee Must be Arraigned**

	Time Within Which Accused Must Be Brought Before Judge	Special Provisions
Alabama		
Alaska	without unnecessary delay, and in any event within 24 hours after arrest (including Saturday, Sunday and holidays)	misdemeanor for officer to refuse to do this, $100 and/ or 30 days
Arizona		an officer or other person who has arrested someone on a criminal charge and wilfully delays taking him before a magistrate is guilty of a misdemeanor
Arkansas	forthwith	
California		an officer or other person who has arrested someone on a criminal charge and wilfully delays taking him before a magistrate is guilty of a misdemeanor
Colorado		
Connecticut	promptly	
Delaware	without unreasonable delay	
Florida		
Georgia	72 hours under warrant; 48 hours without warrant	
Idaho	without unreasonable delay	

Illinois	without unreasonable delay	
Indiana		
Iowa	without unnecessary delay	
Hawaii	48 hours	
Kansas		
Kentucky	without unnecessary delay	
Louisiana		
Miami		
Maryland		
Massachusetts		
Michigan	promptly	magistrate sets a date for preliminary hearing to be held within 10 days
Minnesota		
Mississippi		
Missouri		
Montana	without unnecessary delay	*State v. Johnson,* 307 P. 2d 892 (19) 21-day delay not prejudicial
Nebraska		any officer may detain an arrestee before bringing him before judge one night or longer, "as the occasion may require, so as to answer the purposes of arrest and custody"
Nevada	without unnecessary delay	
New Hampshire	24 hours, unless judge authorizes a 48-hour extension for good cause	

New Mexico		
New Jersey	without unnecessary delay	
New York	without unnecessary delay (but before bringing arrestee to court, police must first fingerprint, photograph and do other preliminary police duties)	where arrest is not for a felony, without an arrest warrant and the police are unable to bring person before a court with reasonable promptness, they must either arrange for pre-arraignment bail or an appearance ticket must be served unconditionally
North Carolina	12 hours if arrested without warrant	misdemeanor for officer to wrongfully delay
North Dakota	without unnecessary delay	
Ohio	without unnecessary delay	
Oklahoma	without unnecessary delay	
Oregon	without delay	
Pennsylvania	without unnecessary delay	persons who have authority to arrest have use of local lockups and prisons for a period of detention not to exceed 48 hours
Rhode Island	24 hours, unless judge orders additional 24 hours for resident, 48 hours for nonresident	
South Dakota	without delay	wilful failure is a misdemeanor

78

	Time Within Which Accused Must Be Brought Before Judge	Special Provisions
South Carolina	reasonable time	
Tennessee		
Texas	without unnecessary delay	
Utah	without unnecessary delay	
Vermont	As soon as practicable	
Virginia	Forthwith	
Washington	Forthwith	
West Virginia	Without unnecessary delay	
Wisconsin		
Wyoming	Without unnecessary delay	

*A blank space indicates no applicable law at the time of this writing.

cases in which people spend days or even weeks in jail without being arraigned. This is, of course, illegal, and it occurs only where the defense lawyers either have no concern for their clients, or are such complacent and un-questioning parts of the system themselves that they do not bring aggressive suits. (A former client of mine was once arrested near Albany, New York, and spent two months in jail on a marijuana charge without being ar-raigned, because the Supreme Court judge was in the midst of a murder trial and would not interrupt it for a five-minute arraignment procedure. The defendant was poor and black.) If you find yourself stuck in jail and cannot get a lawyer who will help you, the only remedy is for you to bring a writ of habeas corpus, discussed in the next chapter.

79

When you are brought to court for arraignment, there should be a lawyer there to represent you. In most large cities, if you are not accompanied by a lawyer, you can be represented by some kind of public defender or legal-aid system. You can have the public defender represent you at the arraignment and still get your own lawyer later; it seems reasonable for you to trust the public defender to handle this part of the proceedings. If she asks you about the facts of the case, it cannot hurt, although it may not help, to tell her anything or everything since by law she cannot reveal what you say to her without your consent. This is called the attorney-client privilege. If there is no lawyer in court to represent you, you should ask for one and you can cite the cases in the beginning of the next chapter in support of your request. If the judge says she will have to postpone the hearing to get a lawyer for you, you can represent yourself. All you have to do, after you are informed of the charges, is give the judge the bail facts (it helps to write them out in advance so you do not forget any), and also tell the judge that you are absolutely reliable and you will definitely appear in court if you are released with or without bail. If you have a record of prior arrests, you can also tell him that on your previous arrests you never missed an appearance. Do not discuss the facts of the case. If the judge asks you about the case, say that you are innocent of the charges, but that you have read a book on what to do if you are arrested and the book advised you not to discuss the case. If you are poor, you should also tell the judge that you will not be able to raise more than a very small bail and you can tell him or her that the Supreme Court has held, in the case of

Stack v. Boyle, 342 U.S. 1 (1951), that great weight must be given to the evidence of reliability and the financial resources of the defendant. As pointed out in the last chapter, it is illegal for the court to set bail in an amount so high that the court knows the defendant cannot post it just to keep the defendant in jail. You can say this to the judge, but you should not be surprised if your argument falls on deaf ears. On the other hand, your argument may have an effect on a fairer judge, who may even be impressed by the legal knowledge of a nonlawyer.

In a few states, notably New York, and in the federal courts, the law has sanctioned preventive detention. That means bail can be denied if an arrestee has a prior record and if there is a substantial amount of evidence against him on the new charge.

RIGHT TO COUNSEL

What are the general rights of a defendant to be represented by a lawyer?

If an accused hires a lawyer, he has the right to have that lawyer with him at any stage of the criminal process from arrest through appeal, except inside a grand jury room. For those who cannot afford a lawyer (perhaps 80 percent of the people arrested), states must furnish a lawyer free of charge to persons accused of felonies, *Gideon v. Wainwright*, 372 U.S. 335 (1963) and, in a recent case, the Supreme Court extended this right to persons accused of misdemeanors in *Argersinger v. Hamlin*, 407 U.S. 25

(1972). Juveniles are also entitled to free counsel where there is a possibility that their freedom will be curtailed, even though the proceedings may be labeled as civil rather than criminal. *In re Gault,* 387 U.S. 1 (1966).

The right to counsel is not limited to the trial itself; it extends to every "critical stage" of the proceedings. As mentioned earlier, when someone is being held for questioning by the police, he has the right to counsel, free if he cannot afford his own, and he must be informed of that right. The right attaches whether or not he is actually in custody, as long as he has somehow been deprived of his freedom in any way. Various Supreme Court decisions have held that defendants have a right to counsel at arraignment, preliminary hearing, on appeal and at hearings on revocation of probation (i.e., probation-violation hearings). A newly developing area of law is whether there is a right to counsel in hearings before parole boards, although presently the rules in almost every jurisdiction are not only that there is no right to counsel, but that a lawyer cannot be present at all even if supplied by the inmate.

What are the mechanics of finding a lawyer in a criminal case?

At the arraignment or the next court appearance, if you appear without your own lawyer, the judge should ask you if you can afford a lawyer and he or she may ask a few questions about your resources. You may be asked about your income, family, bank accounts, the rent you pay, etc. If there are any special circumstances, such as

82

large medical bills, or many children, you should inform the judge of these facts. If you are out on bail, and the bail is a few hundred dollars or more, that fact may be used as a basis for ruling that you can afford a lawyer, so you should be prepared to give the judge reasons why this money is not available to you to pay for a lawyer. Your statements about your resources will generally not be carefully checked; all that may happen is that the judge may want to see a pay stub if you are employed. If he finds that you are indigent (without money or resources), he will appoint a lawyer for you. Where there is a public defender or legal aid society, one of their staff will be appointed. If you can think of some special reason, such as conflict of interest if you are one of two or more defendants, you can request that a lawyer who is not associated with the public defender be appointed for you. It is usually advisable to do this if possible since, even if the public defender is good, two heads are better than one and when one lawyer does something advantageous it usually benefits the other defendant as well. If the judge rules that you are not indigent, he will adjourn the case and tell you to get your own lawyer.

Your family and friends are not obligated to provide a lawyer for you, even if you are under twenty-one, and if they will not provide a lawyer (even after the judge orders you to have your family pay for a lawyer), and you cannot afford one yourself, you are entitled to free counsel.

What happens at a preliminary hearing, and is one always necessary?

Preliminary hearings, which may have different names in different states, are proceedings in which the state must submit a portion, at least, of its case to the court; the court then decides whether there is enough evidence to hold the case for trial. It virtually always consists of a proceeding in which the state's witnesses, police officers or civilians take the witness stand and briefly testify about the facts of the case; then the defense lawyer has a chance to cross-examine the witnesses. Although in theory the preliminary hearing usually is held so that the court can decide whether to hold the case for trial, in practice it is an unsurpassable discovery device for the defense. Virtually all states provide for some form of preliminary hearing.

The value of a preliminary hearing to the defendant is enormous. It informs the defendant of the details of the state's case against him, it gives the defense an opportunity to see the demeanor and testimonial ability of the prosecution witnesses and it provides an opportunity to size up the whole case: to establish whether a guilty plea would be appropriate, or what the chances are to win at trial. Preliminary hearings also have the effect of freezing the testimony of the prosecution witnesses. This means that if the prosecution witnesses testify differently at trial, they can be impeached by introducing into evidence their original testimony at the preliminary hearing. Inconsistencies in the testimony of witnesses at different times are sometimes the strongest part of the defense case. Generally the defendant does not take the stand at a preliminary hearing, since the only purpose this would serve would be to disclose the defense's case to the prosecutor. Preliminary hearings also have the effect of perpetuating testimony: that is, if a witness testifies at a preliminary hearing and subsequently leaves the state, becomes very ill or dies, the testimony of that witness at the preliminary hearing can be used at trial and the witness's presence at the trial will not be necessary. If it is suspected that a witness may not be present at a future trial, then it may be wisest to waive the preliminary hearing. Otherwise, preliminary hearings are very important. Their importance is emphasized here because many lawyers, particularly those in private practice, for whom time is money, do not tell their clients that they have a right to a preliminary hearing and they waive the hearing. The knowledgeable defendant should not permit this.

DISCOVERY

What is discovery, and how is it accomplished?
The criminal procedure laws of almost all states do not provide ways for the defense to find out about the prosecutor's case, except in limited ways. Discovery, as it is called, is vitally important, both for evaluating a case to see if there should be a guilty plea and for preparing a defense.

The best discovery device, the preliminary hearing, has already been discussed. The next best is talking to the prosecution witnesses, both police and civilian. Simple as it sounds, many lawyers do not do it. Some people are under the false impression that talking to prosecution witnesses is not permitted; in fact the canons of ethics in force in most states specifically authorize it. The lawyer or investigator can go to the home of the witness, or the lawyer can have an informal chat with a police officer or civilian witness in the courthouse while waiting for the case to be called. Although many do not know it, prosecution witnesses are under no obligation to talk to the defense. The lawyer sometimes has to use his wits to get the witness to talk, perhaps by telling the witness what the defendant said so that the witness will feel accused of lying and defend himself, or by appearing concerned with the defendant's rehabilitation and saying that he is asking what happened in order to figure out how to help the defendant (which may be true).

The defense can also make a motion for discovery of those items which are available only to the prosecution, and which the defense can prove must be disclosed before trial in order for the defendant to be able to defend himself. Examples of this are: the name and location of any police officers who were with the arresting officer; witnesses who were with a civilian complainant; the prior criminal record of a prosecution witness (available only with fingerprints and from law enforcement agencies); the registered owner of a gun or car; the chemical make-up of a bomb, which would be in the possession of the prosecution (a reason for needing this information could

86

be your allegation that the bomb cannot explode, which makes it not a bomb); any kind of scientific evidence or reports, where the material from which the report is made is in the possession of the prosecution, such as blood tests, ballistics' tests, handwriting, etc. You can even move that the substance be turned over to a laboratory of your choice for another evaluation. Such evidence can be invaluable in preparing a defense, although it usually exists only in more complicated cases. Again, lawyers often do not do enough work on discovery motions; they should be encouraged to do more.

There is one final discovery device, but it is of limited value: a motion for a bill of particulars. This motion has utility where the charges are vaguely stated or where there are many charges and more than one defendant—in which case the defense can move that more details of the charges be disclosed or that the charges against each individual be specified. Courts do not grant motions for bills of particulars where they consider that the information being sought is "evidentiary" in nature, so these motions do not usually yield more than dates, times, and places, and perhaps information about, for example, which defendant is alleged in a murder case to be the trigger man.

Can the defendant obtain the police records of an arrest?

Yes. Documents such as the arresting officer's report of an arrest, his notations in his memorandum book about the case, the complainant's first statement to the police (and even where it exists) and the recording of the complainant's phone call to the police are available to the defense. The method for obtaining this material is simply to serve what is called a subpoena *duces tecum* (a subpoena for records, a form available in stationery stores near courthouses) on the police department.

What is a grand jury, and what is its function?

A grand jury is a group of more than twelve people (the number varies from state to state with the average being perhaps twenty-four) who hears evidence presented by the state in criminal cases, usually in the form of testimony of witnesses, and decides whether the prosecution has enough evidence to charge someone with a crime. If they find enough evidence, they return a list of charges against an individual, and the list of charges is called an indictment. The stated purpose of a grand jury is to protect a citizen from having to undergo the ordeal of a trial when there is not much evidence against him. Although grand juries are supposed to be impartial and representative of the community, they are notoriously lacking in young, poor and minority-group people.

Grand juries today rarely serve their stated purpose. Generally, they act as tools for prosecutors to investigate crime and prosecute those whom they think are criminals. Suspected members of organized crime and members of radical political organizations are often subpoenaed to testify and granted immunity (see below); when they refuse to testify they are charged with contempt of court, which is a felony in many states.

Can the defendant testify before the grand jury, and, if so, is there a right to counsel while testifying?

The rules on this vary from state to state; see Table 7.

Can a citizen who is not a defendant be subpoenaed to testify before a grand jury?

Yes. If this happens to you, you should immediately consult a lawyer. The person subpoenaed can invoke the Fifth Amendment, that is, she can refuse to testify on the grounds that the answer might tend to be incriminating. The government can then either drop the matter or grant the witness immunity, after which the witness can no longer invoke the Fifth Amendment. In the federal system, there are two kinds of immunity: transactional immunity and use immunity. Transactional immunity means that the witness cannot be prosecuted for any crime that the witness is questioned about, while use immunity means only that the government is barred from using the testimony of the witness to find further evidence against that witness; use immunity also means that the grand jury testimony cannot be used against the witness at trial. Use immunity has been upheld as not violative of the Fifth Amendment, although it means that a person may be forced to testify and later prosecuted for crimes testified about.

Table 7

State	Defendant allowed to testify	Defendant allowed to have counsel while testifying	Defendant allowed to testify only if subpoenaed	Defendant not allowed to testify	No law on subject	Comments (see below)
Alabama					X	
Alaska						
Arizona	X	X				1.
Arkansas	X					
California	X					
Colorado				X		
Connecticut						2.
Delaware			X			
Florida			X			
Georgia					X	
Hawaii					X	
Idaho	X					
Illinois				X		
Indiana			X			3.
Iowa	X					
Kansas		X				4.
Kentucky	X					
Louisiana	X					
Maine					X	
Maryland					X	
Massachusetts				X		
Michigan			X			
Minnesota	X					
Mississippi					X	
Missouri					X	
Montana	X					
Nebraska					X	
Nevada	X					

State	Defendant allowed to testify	Defendant allowed to have counsel while testifying	Defendant allowed to testify only if subpoenaed	Defendant not allowed to testify	No law on subject	Comments (see below)
New Hampshire					X	
New Jersey					X	
New Mexico	X					
New York	X					5.
North Carolina					X	
North Dakota	X					
Ohio			X			
Oklahoma	X					
Oregon	X					
Pennsylvania				X		
Rhode Island					X	
South Carolina					X	
South Dakota	X					
Tennessee					X	
Texas	X					6.
Utah	X					
Vermont					X	
Virginia					X	
Washington	X					
West Virginia					X	
Wisconsin					X	
Wyoming					X	

Comments to Table 7

1. *May* hear at his request; if yes, right to counsel.
2. Statute allows defendant to be in grand jury room as matter of privilege, not right, but he may *not* testify.
3. Proposed law: Defendant can testify if he makes written request, signs waiver of immunity; also, grand jury has

91

discretion to hear other witnesses in defendant's behalf on his request.
4. Neither statute nor case law says when defendant has right to testify.
5. Defendant has right to appear upon written request; grand jury has discretion to hear witnesses in his behalf or his request.
6. Statute not clear-cut, but would seem to allow grand jury to question "accused or suspect."

Can a person subpoenaed to testify before a grand jury resist testifying on grounds other than the Fifth Amendment?

Yes, but the likelihood of success is not great. The subpoena may have been improperly given to the witness, the members of the grand jury may have been improperly selected or the questions may involve privileged communications such as those between husband and wife or attorney and client. There are a few other defenses, but all are complicated and require good legal help. One successful defense is that a witness does not have to testify where the information that led to the subpoena came from illegal wiretaps. (*Gelbard v. U.S.*, 408 U.S. 41 [1972].)

Is it advisable for a defendant to testify before a grand jury?

Usually not. Testifying before the grand jury will disclose the defense's case to the prosecution, and anything said to the grand jury can be used to impeach the defendant at trial. Furthermore, most grand juries are prosecution-oriented and almost always follow the recommendations made to them by the district attorney. However, there are certain kinds of cases in some jurisdictions which are often dismissed or reduced to misdemeanors by the grand jury. Charges such as assault on a police officer where there was only a minor scuffle, or possession of a small amount of marijuana, may technically be felonies but the grand jury may refuse to indict, especially if they see the defendant and he claims innocence.

MOTIONS TO EXCLUDE EVIDENCE

What is inadmissible evidence, and how can the defense prevent its use at trial?

When evidence is illegally obtained by the police, it is not admissible at trial. Procedurally the lawyer must make a motion to exclude the evidence, usually in writing, and sometime before trial a hearing is held on the motion. Testimony is taken and cross-examined and legal arguments are made by the lawyers. In possession cases— which involve, for example, drugs or weapons—there may be no dispute about the possession but only about the legality of the search and the motion to suppress the evidence becomes the most important procedure in the case. Chapters I and II describe some illegal police practices in gathering evidence. This section will briefly describe the four most common motions to exclude evidence, a few of the common police responses in such motions and some methods to be explored by the defense in order to win the motion. This information is presented here because there are a great many lawyers who do an inadequate job in preparing such motions, especially in gathering evidence and closely examining the facts, and defendants should know this material themselves.

The most common motion in this area is to suppress physical evidence on the grounds that it was seized during an illegal search by the police without a warrant. If your car or person or home was searched without a warrant and contraband found, this is the motion your lawyer would make. Some of the predictable lies that police officers testify to in order to cover up illegal searches are that the contraband was dropped to the ground by the defendant as the police officer approached him (the "dropsy" story, see page 23); the contraband was in plain view on the person of the defendant (for example, the defendant was smoking a marijuana cigarette while walking down the street, or his coat was open and a gun was visible in his belt); the contraband was in plain view in a car while the police officer was making a routine check of the license and registration of the car (for example, the police officer looked into the car and saw the barrel of a gun sticking out from under the seat or glassine envelopes on the floor); or the contraband was seen by the police officer when he came to a residence occupied by the defendant (for example, when the police officer knocked on the door to tell the occupants to turn their phonograph down, he looked into the apartment and saw drugs on a table). There are innumerable variations, but the themes are similar.

After the police officer testifies, the defendant may take

94

the stand and give his version of the facts. Defendants should be aware that they can testify at a motion to suppress evidence that they possessed the contraband, and, under present case law (which may change), that testimony cannot be introduced at trial. (*Simmons v. U.S.*, 390 U.S. 377 [1968]; but see *Peo. v. Harris*, 28 L. Ed. 2d I [1971].) If the defendant does testify at the motion to suppress, he must say that the contraband was possessed by him; if he testifies that the contraband was planted on him, the judge would rule that the defendant's own testimony is that he is not the victim of an illegal search. However, if the defendant says the contraband was planted, the motion to suppress can actually still be made by simply stating in the motion papers that there was an illegal search (which there must have been if there was a plant), and that the defendant is now charged with possession of the contraband. The police officer's testimony can then be examined to see if it describes an illegal search, which it might, and the defendant need not take the stand.

What can be done to combat police perjury? The methods are the same in this area as in any other, and there is much the client can do to help the lawyer and to help the defense of the case. If an illegal search took place on the street or in an area where there are other members of the public passing by, a thorough search for witnesses should be made. Probably the most powerful defense to police perjury is an independent witness. Occasionally such a witness may be found by distributing leaflets to passersby who were on the street at approximately the same time of day as the time of arrest, and this should be done as soon after the arrest as possible. Also, a detailed examination and perhaps a diagram and/or photograph of the scene of arrest may show either that the police officer could not see what he said he did, or that what he said he saw is so unlikely in the light of ordinary human behavior that it is not believable. For example, the police officer may say he saw drugs being passed from A to B in the doorway to an apartment while he was perched on a stairway landing; a detailed diagram might show that he could not have seen anything but a small part of the door near the hinge. Or he may say he saw drugs passed from A to B on a sidewalk outside a housing project; a diagram of the area might show that the spot is so much in the plain view of the people in apartments, on sidewalks and in the street that the police officer's story is so unlikely that it should not be believed. Note that the person who makes the diagram or takes pictures will have to testify, so it should be someone with at least some training, and he or she should not be either a relative or close friend of the defendant. In addition, the defense should subpoena other police officers present at the time of arrest. Although it is rare that a police officer will testify that another officer conducted an illegal search, this sometimes does happen and, furthermore, your lawyer may be able to find inconsistencies in both their testimonies (on details that they did not rehearse), and this can be evidence of lying.

The police sometimes make mistakes and, by not knowing some fine points, actually testify to an illegal search. If the police testify to a dropsy story, and say that what was dropped was wrapped and that the police officer picked it up right after it was dropped, then his opening of the package was an illegal search unless there was some other basis for it. The reason for this is that the package, which might, for example, be a cigarette pack or eyeglass case, was not apparently abandoned by the defendant when it was picked up; it is therefore still considered part of the defendant's person, and the police officer had the duty to give it back to the defendant, not open it. If the police officer is aware of these rules, he probably would testify that the defendant threw the package away, perhaps into the gutter or into a garbage can, and then the package would be considered apparently abandoned and he could legally open it.

If your home, office, store, etc., was searched with a warrant, the appropriate motion is to controvert the search warrant. As outlined in Chapter II, search warrants can be obtained only upon the police officer showing to the court that there is probable cause to believe that a crime is being committed on a certain premises, that a search will yield evidence of crime; the affidavit must specifically set forth the facts that constitute the probable cause. At the hearing on the motion to controvert the search warrant, the court looks into whether the affidavit contained enough information to give probable cause and also whether the affidavit itself is true. Most affidavits are based on information supplied by informers, and in such cases the Supreme Court has held that the affidavit must contain concrete facts showing that the informant is reliable. This is usually done by a statement to the effect that the informer has given information leading to convictions in other cases without naming those cases. At a motion to controvert a search warrant, your lawyer should get the names of these other cases and check the records of the cases; the police are often sloppy in preparing search warrants, and such an investigation may show that the police officer does not really know of other cases in which the informer's information led to conviction.

Under certain circumstances, the defense can ask the court to direct that the undercover agent be produced in court, perhaps without the presence of the defendant or defense counsel, so that the undercover agent's identity is not revealed. The grounds for such an application are that the evidence presented is so weak that the court should require the undercover agent to affirm the police officer's testimony. Another possible ground is that the undercover agent could supply information that would show that the defendant is innocent. (*Roviaro v. U.S.*, 353 U.S. 53 [1957].) Wherever possible such an application should be made; if it is granted it may lead to dismissal of the case, because undercover agents will often refuse to come to court and if the police officer is lying he will then probably say that the undercover agent will not come to court.

Police officers frequently lie about the information given to them by undercover agents; sometimes their undercover agent, who is often an addict, has not given them any information about the particular defendant, while at other times he or she merely told the police officer that so-and-so was a dealer. The police officer might say in court that the informer told him that he was in the suspect's house, perhaps several times, that he made a buy and that he saw drugs there, and the police officer

98

might say he had several conversations with the informer. The only way to combat this kind of perjury—and it is very difficult to do so successfully—is by a very close, thorough cross-examination. Your lawyer should ask the police officer how many conversations he had with the informer, where he was when the first one took place, where the informer was, who was with him, what the informer said, what he said in response, who else was in the room when the conversations were being held (and they can then be subpoenaed), and so on for each conversation that was alleged to have taken place, including how much the informer bought, what quantity of drugs the informer said he saw, how badly hooked the informer is, what he does for money for drugs, how long he has been an informer, how often the police officer sees the informer, what would happen to the informer if he stopped giving information, where he sees the informer and so forth.

Where the state seeks to introduce any confession or statement against the defendant, the lawyer should always make a motion to suppress the statements on the grounds that they were illegally obtained. Even if the motion cannot succeed, it will reveal what statements will be introduced into evidence at trial. Statements are illegally obtained if they are given by a defendant involuntarily, which can mean that they are induced by psychological pressure or tricks, or threats, as discussed more fully in Chapter III. They are also inadmissible if the defendant was not given his *Miranda* warnings prior to being questioned, i.e., that he has a right to remain silent, that anything he says may be used in evidence against him, and that he has a right to a lawyer, including a free one if he cannot afford one; for the statements to be admissible, the defendant must knowingly waive these rights. Usually it is the police officer's word against the defendant's, and there is not much that can be done, especially if the only witnesses to the questioning are other police officers and perhaps other persons arrested that day who were waiting in the precinct house for transfer to court. Where the issue is whether the defendant was advised of his rights, other police officers may or may not be helpful; they may simply bolster each other's testimony. However, where the defendant's responses to the warnings could indicate absence of a waiver of constitutional rights, or where the length of time of the defendant's interrogation is in issue, other officers who participated or sat in on the interrogation should be subpoenaed. The names of other persons arrested, who may have overheard the manner of questioning, or who may have seen whether the defendant was mistreated and how long he was questioned, can be gotten from a logbook in the precinct house or by a motion for discovery. In trying to show that the waiver of constitutional rights was not done knowingly, it may be helpful to have the police officer read the warnings in court as he read them to the defendant, from start to finish, and perhaps investigate such factors as the defendant's intelligence, his ability to comprehend the warnings (perhaps by psychological tests), language difficulties, and any response he might have given to the warnings. If it is revealed that he said, even once, that he did not want to make a statement or that he wanted to have a lawyer, and the questioning continued and he then made statements, such statements are inadmissible.

Where a lineup or showup was held, the lawyer should always make a motion to suppress evidence of the identification. Again, even if the motion stands little chance of success, it will still serve to give the defense an opportunity to observe the complaining witness and to learn how definite the identification is. The factors that make a lineup or showup illegal are discussed previously in Chapter III. At the hearing on the motion, if there is any possibility of success, the lawyer should subpoena all the other police officers present in order to question them, and make a motion for discovery of the names of all the other persons in the lineup in order to try to duplicate the lineup in court. One frequent and grossly unfair practice in lineups is that the standins are police officers who look significantly different because of facial expression, neatness and posture from ghetto residents and persons who have been arrested. This is very obvious to anyone who works with defendants but, not unexpectedly, judges and district attorneys are either unaware of this fact or ignore it. It may be helpful to have a psychologist view the lineup and testify as an expert that the lineup was suggestive. Again, as in every hearing on a motion, a close, thorough cross-examination should be conducted, whenever appropriate, on the question of whether the defendant was informed of his right to a lawyer and knowingly waived that right. The lawyer can bring out all the details of this event, such as the position of the defendant at the time he was advised of his rights, the position of the police officer, the name and location of everyone else in the room, their positions in the room, exactly what was said to the defendant, exactly what the defendant said in response, whether anyone else said anything and if so what, whether the defendant signed a statement admitting that he was informed of his rights, and if not, whether it isn't a practice to give the defendant a sheet of paper with his *Miranda* warnings on it prior to being questioned, and if that is so why was such a sheet of paper not given to the defendant prior to a lineup, etc.

The preceding paragraphs are a necessarily rough outline of law and tactics in this area. If you are seriously interested in participating in depth in the defense of your case, a decision which is strongly recommended, you are referred to *Busted: A Handbook for Lawyers and Their Clients,* by Oliver A. Rosengart, available from the National Lawyers Guild, 1 Hudson Street, New York, New York; *Law and Tactics in Exclusionary Hearings,* by Thomas P. Abbott and others, Coiner Publishers, Washington, D.C., and *Trial Manual for the Defense of Criminal Cases,* by Anthony Amsterdam and others, American Law Institute. For a useful book on cross-examination, see *The Art of Cross-Examination,* by Francis L. Wellman, Collier Books, New York, New York.

TRIAL AND SENTENCE

After all hearings on motions have taken place, and after all other pre-trial motions are completed (there are many other motions that can be made, but they are almost always done in writing without a hearing), the matter goes to trial. In a book of this kind there is little that can be said about trial, other than directing you to the works mentioned at the end of the previous section.

When does a person have a right to trial by jury?

When the maximum sentence for the offense is more than six months' imprisonment. *Baldwin v. New York,* 399 U.S. 66 (1970).

Is it advisable to waive a jury and go to trial before a judge?

Usually not. Most lawyers agree that juries are significantly more likely to acquit than judges, although there are circumstances where the constituency from which the jury is drawn and the nature of the case are such that a judge trial is more advantageous. Jury trials are much longer than judge trials, since there are opening and closing statements, questioning of the jury, etc., and defendants should beware of lawyers who want to waive a jury in order to save themselves time.

Can a person be convicted of a crime on the uncorroborated testimony of an accomplice?

The rules vary from state to state. Corroboration of an accomplice's testimony is needed in the following states: Alabama, Alaska, Arizona, Arkansas, California, Georgia (in felony cases only), Iowa, Kentucky, Maryland, Minnesota, Montana, New York, North Dakota, Oklahoma, Oregon, Texas, Utah.

Corroboration is not needed—that is, a person can be convicted of a crime solely on the testimony of an accomplice—in the following states: Delaware, Illinois, Indiana, Louisiana, Missouri. The states not mentioned have no rules on the subject, which means that what is called the common law should apply. The common law rule is that corroboration is required, but it is not definite that this is exclusively the rule in the states not mentioned.

Can a man be convicted of rape on the uncorroborated testimony of a woman?

The rules vary from state to state. In the following states corroboration is required: Alabama, Alaska, Connecticut, Georgia, Iowa, Nebraska, New Mexico, New York, North Carolina, Vermont. New York recently changed its law, so that corroboration is required only of an attempt to engage in sexual intercourse and of lack of consent; previously the identity of the alleged rapist also had to be corroborated. Many different kinds of evidence can constitute corroboration, such as a complaint by the victim to a friend, relative or the police immediately after the incident, physical injury, a doctor's examination of the victim immediately after the rape, or another witness seeing the rapist enter the home of the victim.

Many other states have held, by judicial decisions, that corroboration of the victim's testimony is not required. These states are: Arizona, Arkansas, California, Delaware, Florida, Hawaii, Idaho, Illinois, Indiana, Kansas,

Maine, Maryland, Michigan, Minnesota, Missouri, Nevada, New Jersey, Ohio, Oklahoma, Pennsylvania, Rhode Island, South Carolina, South Dakota, Tennessee (where victim is over twenty-one), Texas (except where belated outcry is made), Virginia, Washington, Wisconsin, and Wyoming. However, in these states, if in the course of the trial the evidence shows that the witnesses' testimony is contradictory or unbelievable, then corroboration is necessary to convict.

How can a defendant tell whether he is being properly represented before trial?

When a case goes to trial, the lawyer should be thoroughly prepared. He should be so familiar with the evidence and the witnesses' testimony that it is practically committed to his memory. He should have visited all areas about which there will be testimony; he should have conducted thorough interviews with witnesses for the defense, and, wherever possible, the lawyer should have either a brief or photocopies of cases or textbooks on the disputed subjects. If he has prepared well, he will have looked for other witnesses and considered the advisibility of using expert witnesses to duplicate the events, or testify about the impossibility of some prosecution evidence. Also, the lawyer's materials should be organized for easy access in court. If it is not clear that all of these preparations are being made, ask the lawyer about it and keep asking him until you are satisfied that your case is being properly prepared; most lawyers are overworked and they will attend to matters that they are constantly reminded about

105

more than other matters. If he or she seems thoroughly neglectful or passive, get another lawyer. The best way to get quality legal services is to learn as much as you can about what constitutes good representation, and then insist on it.

How can a defendant best prepare for sentencing?

Should you lose a trial or plead guilty you will, of course, face sentencing, which can consist of anything from a suspended sentence to a fine, probation, or jail time. In almost all states there is an adjournment between the time of conviction and the time of sentencing, so you will have an opportunity to prepare for sentence. There are many forms this preparation can take. Some judges respond positively to the presence of many people, especially semi-establishment types, appearing in court on the defendant's behalf, so such people should be rounded up and prepared to spend the day of the sentencing in court. In addition, letters should be solicited from teachers, counselors, therapists, employers, etc. The letters should show the context in which the writer knows the defendant, as well as his estimate of the defendant's character and ability to stay out of trouble in the future. They should be sent to the judge and to the probation department, which generally prepares the pre-sentence report for the judge. Courts are essentially middle-class institutions, and judges usually respond positively to a defendant's participation in middle-class rehabilitative activities. Thus, it may help if, between conviction and sentencing, the defendant gets a job, goes back to school, enrolls in a

106

drug program of any kind, starts supporting his mother, gets married or brings any children he or she has to court on sentencing day. At the time of sentencing, it may also be helpful for the defendant to bring his psychotherapist or social worker to court and the defendant should dress as neatly as possible. In some cases it is helpful to have the lawyer make a personal statement, in which he says that he has gotten to know the defendant personally and gives his own estimate of the defendant's character. Needless to say, do not get yourself arrested just before sentencing.

IV

Remedies

This will be a short chapter, because the remedies that exist to counteract police misconduct are few, and in the final analysis they do not work, except in occasional situations.

THE COURTS

What can a defendant do if he is arrested and not brought to court for arraignment?

The best and fastest remedy is by writ of habeas corpus. This is a proceeding in which you submit to the judge a petition, which is nothing more than a statement by you, and an order for the judge to sign. The order directs the jailer to bring you before the judge and to show cause why you should not be released or the conditions of your detention changed, in this case by having bail set. Sample forms of a writ and petition for writ are given on pages 119–22. Federal law and virtually all state laws provide that the judge must sign the writ (the order directing that you be

111

brought to court), which means that you must be brought before the court, although of course the judge can refuse to grant you the relief you are seeking.

The papers can be drawn up in any manner on any kind of paper, typed or in pencil. A simple letter to a judge from an inmate is supposed to be considered as a writ. The petition can be made in affidavit form and signed before a notary public, if one is available to prisoners (occasionally they are), but this is not necessary. The return date (the date the order directs that you be brought before the judge) should be the next day. You should give the papers to the jailer and demand that they be brought to the judge. If he refuses, tell him that the Constitution so requires, and that you will sue him for false imprisonment and violation of constitutional statutory rights if he does not deliver the papers. If he still refuses, try mailing them or smuggling them out with someone who is leaving. Writs of habeas corpus can also contest other illegal conditions of detention, such as cruel and inhuman treatment (a violation of the Eighth Amendment) if there are beatings, inedible food, etc. Needless to say, such suits rarely meet with success, which does not mean they should not be brought; they may have some coercive effect on the jailer just because he will be brought to court, and they may have political value within the prison.

How can a citizen obtain relief from the courts for specific police misconduct?

Where citizen's individual rights (those described in

112

Chapter II) are violated—where, for example, there has been an illegal search or illegal questioning—the courts are generally useless as a means for bringing about change. Where there has been an arrest, the citizen can only assert, on a motion to suppress, that his rights have been violated defensively and if he succeeds the case may be dismissed, but no sanctions will have been applied against the police and the illegal conduct will continue. In addition, such motions are decided by judges without a jury, and, as has been mentioned before, many are notoriously biased. If the motion to suppress is successful, or if no arrest followed the police misconduct, the citizen could theoretically bring a civil lawsuit against the police officer and the local government. However, such suits are a waste of time: if there is no arrest, then there is no damage that will be compensable, and if there is an arrest, the policeman will probably lie again in the civil suit, the defendant would have the burden of proof, and the jury probably would believe that he was a criminal and would not want to award him monetary damages from the municipal treasury. A suit to enjoin the police from illegally searching or questioning people, which would be decided by a judge without a jury, presents virtually impossible problems of proof and has little chance of success.

Where there has been a beating and an injury, a suit for monetary damages against the police officer and the municipality can be effective. In one recent year, New York City paid out a total of $169,482 on 35 claims for money damages for injuries caused by police.* Although

*Walter Gellhorn, *When Americans Complain* (Cambridge: Harvard University Press, 1966), p. 184.

obviously, most such suits are not successful and therefore few are instituted, they should be brought, since the police are extremely sensitive about civil suits, and the very existence of the suit can often coerce at least that particular police officer into proper conduct in the future.

The most pervasive form of police misconduct is perjury in court, and it continues unchecked and unthreatened. The practice is supported by other police officers who corroborate their co-workers' testimony, and who would severely ostracize any policeman who violated police solidarity on this issue. It is also supported by district attorneys who do not prosecute policeman for perjury even when they know the policeman is lying, and by the judges who generally accept perjured police testimony.

ADMINISTRATIVE COMPLAINTS

What about complaining to a police review board?

Most police departments have some office or board for processing complaints from the public. They are almost always staffed by members of the police department. In New York City, the Civilian Complaint Review Board is aggressive only against policeman who commit assaults, or commit other serious crimes, and they seem to operate along the general rule that where it is the policeman's word against the civilian's, the policeman's version is accepted no matter how credible the civilian's complaint. Where the police misconduct consists of illegally searching or questioning someone, complaints to the police depart-

114

ment or any other agency are usually a waste of time. However, where the misconduct is an assault or other crime, the complaint should be made because of its deterrent effect. Some larger cities have special investigating agencies that will look into serious police criminal activity, such as selling drugs or accepting bribes. These agencies vary so much from city to city, and so much depends on the personalities of their leaders and staffs, that it is impossible to discuss them here in detail.

POLITICAL SOLUTIONS

In the final analysis, the problem of police misconduct goes to the roots of our society. We live in a country with an enormous amount of crime on all socioeconomic levels; why should the police be different? Like most of society, the police are dissatisfied and alienated; they resent the lack of dignity in their work and the lack of respect society has for them. They resent much of the job they have been given, because part of it is to mop up the casualties of society's neglect of one quarter of the population, to contain the fifty million or so have-nots and to preserve the status quo for the haves. The authoritarian nature of the work attracts politically conservative individuals who oppose political change and political activism. It may be trite, but it must be said: that the only real answer to the problem of police misconduct is a more socially and economically just society.

The instigation of some immediate changes would be a beginning, although they are politically very difficult to impose. These include: a system of psychological testing to weed out the small number of authoritarian, repressed, policeman who are attracted to police work only because of the opportunities for violence and racism that the work offers; massive recruiting of minority-group people for the police force; and real community control of the police— that is, control by the local community where the police are working, not by the local municipality. And most importantly, the police need a great deal of education about the nature of society, why it is so badly split, why the resources are so unevenly distributed and why we have so much crime on all levels. Police should be taught the psychology of crime, how crime is often an adaptation to a horrible environment and to a feeling of powerlessness, as well as the psychological meaning of drug use, not just its behavior. And the police should be exposed to the life background and conditions of criminals, so that they might understand that except for luck the person the police officer arrests could be himself or you or me.

Appendix

SAMPLE WRIT AND PETITION FOR WRIT OF HABEAS CORPUS
SUPREME COURT OF THE STATE OF NEW YORK
COUNTY OF THE BRONX
PEOPLE OF THE STATE OF NEW YORK
EX REL
ON BEHALF OF

against

ARTHUR J. SINGERMAN, WARDEN OF BRONX
HOUSE OF DETENTION FOR MEN,
                    Defendant

To: ARTHUR J. SINGERMAN, Warden of the Bronx House of Detention for Men.
Greeting:

WE COMMAND YOU, that you have and produce the body of the said   by you imprisoned and detained, as it is said, together with your full return to this writ, and the time and cause of such imprisonment and detention by whatsoever name the said person shall be called or charged before Hon.   one of the Justices of the Supreme Court of the state of New York, county of the Bronx at Part I, 851 Grand Concourse, Bronx, New York in the courthouse thereof on the   day of   , 19   at 10:00 A.M. to do and receive what shall then and there be considered concerning the said person and have you then and there this writ.

119

WITNESS, Hon.   one of the Justices
of our said Court, the   day of   , 1970
                                  Clerk
                                  Name and address of attorney
The within writ is hereby allowed this   day of   ,
19
To the Honorable Supreme Court of the State of New York,
County of the Bronx.
The Petition of   , by his attorney,
                             , respectfully shows:

1. I am an attorney admitted to the Bar of this Court with
office at   , City,
County and State of New York, and I am counsel to   ,
the defendant herein.

2.   is detained at the Bronx
House of Detention for Men, and the officer by whom he is
detained is   , Warden of the said
House of Detention.

3. The cause or pretense for the detention of
is that he is charged in the Criminal Court, Bronx County,
with the crimes of felonious assault, possession of a dangerous
weapon, resisting arrest, and the violation of disorderly conduct.
He is alleged to have assaulted a police officer on
                            at   and a
copy of the charges is attached as Exhibit A. No preliminary
hearing has been held.

4.   is held by virtue of mandates of
the Criminal Court setting his bail at $. He has
been so detained since   , and two applica-
tions for reduction of bail have been made in Criminal Court,
both of which have been denied.

5. This bail of   is excessive and arbitrary,
and the incarceration of   , by reason of
such bail terms is in violation of his rights under the New York
State Constitution, Article I, Section 5 and the United States
Constitution, Amendments 8 and 14.

6. The relator has been detained since   , 19 ,
without a preliminary hearing, on information and belief because the prosecutor proposed to bring this case before the

120

Grand Jury and foreclose a hearing. At the last adjourned day of this case in Criminal Court,   , 19   , the prosecutor said that he was not ready, although the arresting officer, who is the complaining witness, was present and able to testify. The relator is being held while the People seek to circumvent CCP §190.

7. Bail may only be used to insure the appearance of the defendant and not for detention. In this case, the character, background and circumstances of relator are such that there is no difficulty in insuring his appearance if he is released. He is twenty-one years old and lives with his mother and family at   . At the time of his arrest, he was in the U.S. Army. He had just completed thirteen months of duty, including a tour in Vietnam, on information and belief under honorable conditions, and he was on leave. I have spoken to Captain   of the Judge Advocate General's office in Fort Wadsworth and he has informed me that the Army will arrange to have the defendant return for his court appearances. He is not due to be sent overseas, since he has just returned from Vietnam. Captain further stated that if this Court ordered that the relator not leave the confines of the City of New York, the Army would arrange to station him here. Mr.   has previously been convicted of being a youthful offender, but, on information and belief, he never showed any propensity to avoid the orders of the court or to fail to appear in that proceeding.

8.   vehemently denies guilt of the charges against him. He does not wish to flee the jurisdiction but rather to stay and establish his innocence. The events at issue in this case occurred in   , when the offender tried to have the relator and others leave the park, and an altercation ensued. The officer subsequently shot twice, once through the body and once in the leg. He then shot a co-defendant,   , who is now free on $2500 bail. He has arrested both and   , and on   , 1969, he arrested in court one   , a bystander at the altercation and a friend of the defendant's family. It

121

is submitted that the circumstances of this case raise serious issues as to the guilt or innocence of the defendant.

9. On information and belief, the present bail of is beyond the means of the relator's family. His mother and her family are supported by welfare payments. The present bail acts solely as a means of retaining the relator in jail, and punishing him without trial.

10. No court or judge of the United States Government has exclusive jurisdiction to order released.

11. No previous application for the relief requested herein has been made.

WHEREFORE, your petitioner prays that an order issue, reducing the bail heretofore fixed to the sum of
STATE OF NEW YORK)
COUNTY OF NEW YORK) SS:

, , being duly sworn, deposes and says that he is the petitioner in this proceeding, that he has read the foregoing petition, and the same is true to his knowledge except for those portions alleged to be on information and belief, and as to those, he believes them to be true.
Sworn to before me this
day of , 1970.
Petitioner

OLIVER ROSENGART is an assistant professor at New York University, teaching in the Metropolitan Studies Program. After law school, Mr. Rosengart worked as a criminal lawyer at Mobilization for Youth, an antipoverty program on New York's lower east side. He then taught for three years at New York University Law School in the Criminal Law Clinic, where he continued to represent indigent defendants, and he supervised law students in their representation of indigent defendants. He was for five years a part-time tenant organizer with the Metropolitan Council on Housing, a tenant organization, and has worked with the National Lawyers Guild. His other publications are *Busted: A Handbook for Lawyers and Their Clients* and *A Brief Introduction to Cross-Examination.*